The Rise of the Roman Empire:

Life, Liberty, and the Death of the Republic

By Barry Linton

Copyright 2015 by Barry Linton.

Published by Make Profits Easy LLC

Profitsdaily123@aol.com

facebook.com/MakeProfitsEasy

Table of Contents

Foreword 4

Chapter 1: Foundation of Rome 12

Chapter 2: Carthage and the Punic Wars 32

Chapter 3: Vacuum of Power 71

Chapter 4: The Triumvirate 93

Chapter 5: Civil War in Rome 132

Chapter 6: Death of the Republic 145

Chapter 7: Reigns of Terror 156

Chapter 8: The Collapse 170

Chapter 9: Five Good Emperors 176

Chapter 10: Rome in Crisis 187

Chapter 11: End of the Empire 200

Conclusion 209

Foreword

Rome is everywhere in our culture. It's reflected in our films, in our religions, in our laws, and in our very language. While the Roman Empire as we have come to know it no longer exists, what remains of their awe-inspiring legacy has been left behind across three continents. Images and texts still exist along with the many great structures of this ancient culture. The images, sights, and sounds of the fervent uproar of Roman culture are ingrained in the minds of people everywhere.

Even as a commentary on the nature of man, the life and times of ancient Rome is fascinating and often thrilling. It began as nothing more than a small group of settlements along the River Tiber in central Italy, and there were many rivals only a few short kilometers away. In time Rome conquered the entire peninsula and even grew powerful enough to destroy Carthage in North Africa. Rome continued to grow and eventually pursued a course of conquest that would span the Mediterranean Sea and into modern-day France and Britain. Eventually these and more were brought into the fold of the Roman civilization, leaving their mark forever. Rome impresses with its innovations, many unique and unheard-of in that time. Rome sought to grow and much of its success is owed to its policy of extending citizenship to the peoples that they conquered. Vastly different cultures were combined and their histories and values added to. This resulted in an empire consisting of many peoples of many different religions and many different races.

    Administering to such a vast empire was incredibly difficult made even more difficult by the ambitions of military dictators and politicians. The Roman world was in nearly constant upheaval over the span of its life, with many struggles between great leaders. Drama was high and larger-than-life figures like Caesar and Pompey or even Antony and Cleopatra played important roles in the fate of this great land. Eventually Octavian rose to power and became the first Roman Emperor and one by one introduced a new system of laws whose influence is felt even today. Much of the success of that period and the laws that have been handed down depended upon the character and good intentions of that one individual. There were many good emperors who intended good things for their people, but the growth and stability of Rome was offset by the madness and turmoil brought by bloodthirsty tyrants like Nero or even Caligula. But even with the setbacks, the Roman Empire continued to flourish.

Many new cities rose and older ones grew and were improved. Every part of the Empire was linked by a network of roads, completely unheard of in other parts of the world previous to this. The Romans were masters of innovation bringing sewer systems and vast networks of water supplies to their cities. Great feats of architecture and public works were created and came to define Roman life. Common to most major Roman cities were public baths, circuses, temples, and forums to speak your mind. Perhaps the most well-known structure of all, the Coliseum, stood stark and massive against the Roman skyline. It brought wealth and spectacle while gladiators fought and died for entertainment and glory. Houses and other tenements dotted the countryside and filled every street. Rome also brought rise to Townhouses and country villas. Culture flourished in Rome and through them the borrowed Greek culture lived on and was added to with great Roman contributions of arts, literature, philosophy, and magnificent architecture. Rome has a great history of incorporating elements from every culture combined into it and making them truly Roman.

Beginning in the third century A.D. and onward, peace within this empire was increasingly threatened by many conflicts between political rivals and emperors, and the borders were pressed upon, forcing the Legion to fiercely attempt to defend. The Imperial borders were pressured by barbarian tribes and raiders, and warfare ensued nearly constantly. While the political history of Rome is tumultuous, Rome was known for its resiliency and it managed to survive even while massive and widespread changes occurred within it, culminating in the adoption of Christianity which eventually became its exclusive religion. Finally by the fifth century, the Empire of Rome broke into pieces and completely collapsed in the West by 476 when the last Emperor abdicated his throne. In the East, the Roman Empire continued to live on for another thousand years in the form of the Byzantine Empire. The influences of Rome are far-reaching and even with the fall of these successors, Roman reach is still felt today. Rome has indelibly left its mark upon many civilizations and their very histories to this day.

The history of Rome's rise was slow and methodical, like all great things taking time for the true shape to appear. Their early history is defined by driving out their kings and developing the Republic. It is this Republic that led to the great conquests that built the Empire. Without their Republic, none of the great expansion and combining of cultures could have taken place. When Rome defeated Carthage, they became master of the Western Mediterranean. Their eyes soon turned to Greece and to Egypt and they made them into Roman provinces, bringing their people and the unique flavor of their way of life into the fold.

Julius Caesar, the great statesman and conqueror, expanded the Roman Empire, their borders, and rule far beyond the Mediterranean into northwestern Europe. The magnitude of these successes are monumental. All of this occurred within 500 years and is a testament to their dedication and unbreakable tenacity that they accomplished this much. It is a testament to the martial skill and might of the well-trained Roman legions. For the majority of its history

Roman legionaries were unbeatable in the field of battle, known for their organization, supreme training doctrines, and the resulting effectiveness in the battlefield. Rome was essentially the first great superpower of the world, yet despite this complicated yet seemingly stable Republican institution, cracks began to appear in the foundations.

There were dire consequences and soon civil war broke out, finally resulting in a single man taking the throne and becoming the first of the Roman emperors. That man was Augustus. The Empire continued to fair exceedingly well and its culture spread, ruled by laws and enforced by the same. By the third century A.D. the Roman Empire was put under increasingly intense pressure. And by the fourth century Christianity became the primary state religion. Finally the empire was put under immense strain, fighting to hold the borders from invading German tribes. These Germanic tribes looted and killed, ran wild, and even sacked Rome. The

Western Roman Empire ended in 476, its puppet ruler leaving his throne of power behind. The Roman Empire in a way lived on in the Greek-speaking Eastern empire, which in many ways was a Roman state for nearly 1,000 years more.

This book is by no means a complete account of everything that happened in Roman history, but the aim is to highlight and explain the culture and the significant events that shaped the influential Empire and ultimately led to its downfall.

Chapter 1: Foundation of Rome

The origins of Rome are humble, beginning as nothing more than a group of hilltop villages. Yet it was this very location upon the hilltop that initially proved key to their survival. It was easily defensible against intruders who in many cases ventured through the marshy low lands populating the area around the river Tiber. The site of this foundation of Rome was eventually known as the famous Seven Hills. And over time it proved to have even greater advantages. The location of this foundation of the Empire proved to be key because it allowed them to control the fastest and most convenient north-south route across the Tiber River. Their location was just over 16 miles from the sea. This placed them in the key position to seek out and control trade with central Italy. This settlement on those famous Romans Seven Hills appears to have started back in the 10th century BC. Many Latin-speaking groups soon moved to the area. They initially occupied and settled the land known as Latium, located south of the Tiber River. The settlements began to grow and by the seventh century BC, villages began to join together. In the Valley between the great hills of Palatine and Esquiline, a great Civic Center was constructed and utilized.

Great Roman traditions that we know today date back to the foundation of the city in 753 BC. The foundation of Rome is credited to two brothers known in history as Romulus and Remus. Rome was founded by Romulus and initially filled and populated by fugitives and outlaws from the surrounding territories. It is written that next he stole women from the neighboring Sabines. At first it might seem plausible, as in many ways it takes after Greek myths. Greek culture is known for its great influence over Roman thinking and development. Even later the legend grew and attached Rome and Greek history together by giving Romulus a distinguished ancestor who is known to be the son of the War God Mars. This ancestor dates back to the Greek siege of the city of Troy which lasted for 10 years. When the Greeks finally breached the Trojan walls using a massive wooden horse with Greek warriors hidden inside of it, the people were slaughtered and the city was destroyed. In one Roman legend however, one of the princes, known as Aenas, eventually escaped and found his way traveling to Italy. He later married the daughter of King Latinus and became that ancient ancestor of the Roman people.

There are several variations on the basic legendary tale. Plutarch presents Romulus and Remus' ancient lineage from Prince Aeneas, fugitive from Troy following its destruction by the Achaeans. Their maternal grandfather is his descendant Numitor, who then inherits the kingship of Alba Longa. Numitor's sibling Amulius inherits its treasury, such as the silver brought by Aeneas from Troy. Amulius utilizes his control of the treasury to dethrone Numitor, but fears that Numitor's child, Rhea Silvia, will bear children who then could overthrow him.

Amulius forces Rhea Silvia into perpetual virginity as a Vestal priestess, but she bears children regardless. In one variation of the tale, Mars, God of War, seduces and impregnates her: in another, Amulius himself seduces her, as well as in yet another, Hercules. The king sees his niece's pregnancy and confines her. She provides birth to two twin brothers of remarkable beauty; her uncle purchases her death and theirs. One account holds that he has Rhea buried alive - the typical punishment for Vestal Virgins who violated their vow of celibacy - and attributes the loss of the twins to exposure to the harsh elements; both means would avoid his direct blood-guilt.

    In an additional tale, he has Rhea and her twins thrown into the depths of the River Tiber. In most variations, a servant is faced with the deed of killing the twins, but cannot bring himself to carry out the nefarious deed. He places them in a basket and leaves it on the river bank for the Tiber to carry. The river rises in a flood and brings the twins downstream, unharmed. The river deity Tiberinus makes the basket catch within the branches of a fig tree that grows in the Velabrum swamp upon the base of the Palatine Hill. The twins are located and suckled by a she-wolf. A shepherd of Amulius named Faustulus discovers them and takes them to his hut, where he and his spouse Acca Larentia raise them as if they were their very own children. In an additional variant, Hercules impregnates Acca Larentia and marries her off to the shepherd Faustulus. She then has twelve sons; whenever one of them dies, Romulus takes his place to found the priestly college of the Arval brothers: Fratres Arvales. Acca Larentia is therefore identified with the Arval goddess Dea Dia, who is worshiped by the Arvals.

In a later Republican religious tradition, a Quirinal priest impersonated Romulus to conduct funerary rites for his foster mother. Another and most likely belated tradition has Acca Larentia as a sacred prostitute (one of several Roman slangs for prostitute was lupa (she-wolf). Still another tradition relates that

Romulus and Remus are nursed by the Wolf-Goddess Lupa or Luperca inside her cave-lair. Luperca was worshiped for the protection she gave sheep from wolves and her partner ended up being the Wolf-and-Shepherd-God Lupercus, who brought fertility to the flocks. She's been identified with Acca Larentia.

In nearly all variations of the story, the twins grew up as shepherds. They arrived into conflict with the shepherds of Amulius, engaging in battles in which Remus was captured and taken to Amulius, under the accusation of being a thief. His true identity was then discovered. Romulus raised a band of shepherds to liberate his brother; Amulius was killed and Romulus and Remus were conjointly offered the throne. They declined it while their grandfather lived, and refused to reside within the town as his subjects.

They restored Numitor as king, paid due respects to their mother Rhea and left to acquire their own town, along with a motley band of fugitives, runaway slaves, and any who wanted fresh opportunities in a new city with brand new rulers. The brothers argued over the best location for the new town. Romulus favored the Palatine Hill; Remus wanted the Aventine Hill. They decided to select the site by divine augury, and each retired to their respective hills and prepared a sacred altar; signs had been delivered to each in the form of vultures or eagles.

Remus saw six; Romulus saw twelve, and reported that his superior vision was because he had the right to rule. Remus made a counterclaim: he saw his six vultures first. Romulus set to work with his supporters, digging a trench across the Palatine to define his town boundaries. Remus criticized some areas of the work and obstructed others from working. At last, Remus leaped over the boundary, as an insult to the city's defenses and their creator. For this offense, he was then killed.

Livy provides two versions of Remus' death. Within the one that is generally better received, Remus criticizes and belittles the brand new defensive fortifications, and in a final insult to the new city and its founder (his brother) alike, he leaps over it. Romulus kills him, saying "So perish every one that shall hereafter leap over my wall".

In the other variation, Remus is simply stated as dead; no murder is alleged. Two other stories record Remus being killed by a blow to the back of the head with a spade. The fatal blow was delivered either by Romulus's commander Fabius or by a man called Celer. Romulus then buries Remus with honor and regrets his brother's death. Romulus completes his town and names it Roma after himself. Then he divides his fighting males into regiments of 3000 infantry and 300 cavalry, which he calls "legions". From the rest of the population he selects 100 of the most noble and wealthy men to serve as his council. He calls these men Patricians: they're fathers of Rome, not only simply because they care for their own genuine citizen-sons but simply because they have actually a fatherly care for Rome and all of its individuals. They are also its elders, and therefore are known as Senators. Romulus therefore inaugurates a system of government and social hierarchy in line with the patron-client relationship.

The ideal of Rome draws in the exiled, the refugees, the dispossessed, criminals and even runaway slaves. The town expands its boundaries to support them. Five of the Seven Hills are settled: the Capitoline Hill, the Aventine Hill, the Caelian Hill, the Quirinal Hill, and the Palatine Hill. Because so many of these immigrants are men, Rome finds itself with a shortage of marriageable women. After following the suggestion of his grandfather Numitor, Romulus holds a solemn event honoring Neptune and invites the neighboring Sabines and Latins to attend; they arrive en masse with their daughters. The Sabine and Latin women who happen to be virgins - 683 according to the record – are then kidnapped and taken back to Rome where they're forced to marry Roman men.

The Greek aspects of these stories aren't surprising because of how pervasive that culture was in the very foundations of Rome. The Greeks themselves were established in Italy during the eighth century and they strongly influenced the Etruscan culture who in turn dominated north central Italy with their large city states. Arguably one of the most important things that the Etruscans acquired from the Greeks was their alphabets and writing. This is important because they then passed it on to the Romans.

In the seventh century, an Etruscan named Tarquinius Priscinus is alleged to have become the king of Rome and for many following centuries there were Etruscan and Etruscan related rulers of Rome. It was during this vital period that Rome began its meteoric rise. Rome became the most powerful city in Latium and by 600 BC it dominated its main rival Alba Longa. Another important introduction brought by the Etruscan kings were early civil amenities. Rome later became famous for these: Public sewer systems that spanned the course of entire cities, multiple temples, some of whom were dedicated to Jupiter, Juno, and Minerva. Eventually Rome was freed from Etruscan control. This occurred around 510 BC and at the same time Rome became a republic. The final Etruscan ruler of Rome was known as Tarquinius Superbus and he was driven from Rome and a revolt led by Lucius Junius Quintus. Tarquinius has been depicted as a tyrant.

Following his expulsion from power, Rome was at war for nearly 2 1/2 centuries. However, important and fundamental institutions were being created. These institutions would define and support the state of Rome for the rest of its history. At first at least, the Roman Republic was ruled by the upper classes. They were known as patricians and they alone were allowed to serve as public officials. Two consuls held chief executive power and they were elected yearly in a large assembly and were generally controlled by the patricians. In times of great need and dire emergency, a special officer could be elected. This was known as a dictator and he was given absolute power for the length of the emergency, but was expected to relinquish that power as soon as the emergency ended. It is evident in Roman history that this did not always occur as planned. As an additional arm of the government, a Senate of elders ruled over legislation.

It is likely that the patricians were originally made up of the wealthy class of citizen, and by the times of the Republic they had become an aristocratic caste. In the majority of cases they were completely unwilling to allow even the richest members of the lower plebeian class into their fold. Balance was maintained however because these ruling patricians were dependent on their so-called inferiors for military manpower. Thus the plebeians were able to force certain concessions. Overall, the struggle between classes remained remarkably peaceful. The main tool employed by the plebeians was called secession, and in essence it meant that the plebeians would leave the city en masse. There is evidence that this happened on multiple occasions from 494 BC onward.

Eventually access to these institutions were reinstated for both the plebeians and patricians. The plebeians were represented by elected tribunes and also had a say in assembly. Patricians had no choice but to accept this integration into the political system because ultimately the power rested with the people, not with the ruling elite, for without them there is no one to rule. Elected tribunes had the power to veto many decisions. The assembly of the people could also pass resolutions that have the power, effect, and full force of law. Eventually plebeians were allowed to serve in all offices and even appeared in the Senate itself. This is one of the most unique elements of Rome, the fact that literally any free citizen could advance their station.

In theory at least Rome would become the state where the people ruled, but often in practice the wealthy and well-born continued to dominate the political sphere. Political life was costly however, which limited those plebeians who could participate in it. Only the richer plebs had much success and soon created a broader ruling class with the patricians. Many resentments arose, but these were deftly diffused by the ruling class through reforms and this led to the growing success of Rome. Previously harsh laws penalized those carrying debt and this was alleviated. New land was frequently colonized and made available by Roman conquest.

Above all however, the Romans proved themselves time and again to be capable of setting aside their differences and banding together in times of crisis. This united front lasted even in the longest of wars that were beset by disappointing defeats. Once Rome was established as a Republic, however, it was unable to maintain dominance in Latium. Eventually this led to accepting other cities in the region as equal partners in a Latin league. Gradually in the course of the fifth century BC, Romans gained the upper hand. The Romans warded off many common enemies of the people and eventually conquered the neighboring Sabine peoples.

In the fourth century Etruscan power had begun to decline. In 396 the neighboring Etruscan city rival was destroyed, relieving Rome from a military and commercial threat. Etruscan cities were self sabotaged by an inability to work together. The United Romans began to destroy them bit by bit. However the Romans themselves experienced a dire setback that could have destroyed them were it not for their resiliency. In 390, a horde of Celtic invaders swiftly invaded from the north. The defending Roman army was defeated. This allowed the capitol of Rome to be captured, and it was subsequently sacked. To Rome's credit, the city was rebuilt and became stronger than ever. Rome reasserted itself as a center of power in the region and dominated leadership of the Latin league. Eventually those once held as equal partners became subordinates. This was severely resisted, but in the Latin war of 342 - 338 BC, Rome emerged the victor. Another half-century of warfare followed. The Samnites, a fierce tribe of mountain fighters, formed alliances with the Etruscans and Gauls. This threatened the very survival of Rome. While generally very successful, Rome at times suffered humiliating and often unexpected defeats. In a battle that took place at the Caudine Forks, the Roman forces allowed themselves to be trapped in a narrow passage and were forced to surrender. Rome itself survived and fought on and once again proved themselves to be successful. Just before the close of the second Samnite war, Romans began to build the great roadway known as the Appian Way. This roadway stretched from the capitol to as far south as Capua. This roadway strengthened and enriched Rome with trade from other fertile regions. The Romans eventually secured Campania after emerging victorious in the Third Samnite war. The Romans pushed northward and crushed uprisings among the Etruscans and Gauls. Soon they built colonies of citizens among them. It seems that nothing could halt the expansion of

Rome. The two greatest qualities of Rome (and the source of their expansive power) was their ability to endure and the ability to recover from nearly any catastrophe. This, above even their military strength, allowed them to inexorably spread across the globe. Generals might win a victory in battle, but the Romans won wars.

The time of the Republic is often seen by writers and historians as being the Golden age, filled with Roman patriots devoted to their duty and their country. One man who perfectly represents this love of country more than self is Cincinnatus. He was a farmer who in a dire emergency was asked to become a dictator, saved Rome within 16 days, and then immediately relinquished his power and went back to farming.

Another source of Rome's long-term success was that Rome was extremely generous in its treatment of allies and conquered enemies. Even as far back as 380 BC, Rome would extend citizenship and rights to their allies and some of their former enemies. This bolstered their numbers, but also built a stable foundation for the Empire. Rather than attempting to eradicate a rival culture and values, Rome would welcome them into the fold and integrate their unique qualities. This stands as a stark contrast to many other would be Empire builders of the time. On the other hand, Rome did not always extend this opportunity. Against the most heated of enemies, Rome proved to be merciless, unafraid to massacre or enslave the defeated so that they may never again pose a threat to Rome. The practice of planting in developing colonies of Roman and Latin settlers brought many new strategic territories to Rome. This ensured that there were always loyal contingents even among their still hostile defeated enemies.

    While a reconciliation with former enemies did not always occur as often or as quickly as might be prudent, it is a testament to Roman foresight and wisdom that it even occurred at all. This willingness to reconcile proved crucial in the future in the many wars against Carthage, when Rome's Italian allies came to their aid. Early on in the third century BC Carthage had not yet become Rome's enemy. When the Romans expanded to the southward, they were brought into direct conflict with the Greeks in Southern Italy. The Romans and Carthaginians were sometimes brought together against them by mutual interests. Carthage itself had often competed against the Greeks in maritime trading. Previously, the Etruscans had helped them keep the Greeks at bay. Control of Sicily was split between Carthage and the Greeks when centuries of struggle accomplished only a stalemate. The Greek state of Tarentum grew suspicious of Roman encroachments. They also felt threatened by the anti-Greek activities of the Carthaginians and Lucanians. Another Greek city-state called Thurii was threatened by the Lucanians and in 282 they asked Rome for help, who sent a military unit that was later used as a garrison.

However, the Tarentines had grown so suspicious and felt so threatened by the Romans that they drove out the Garrison, sank a Roman fleet, and then proceeded to hire Pyrrhus of Epirus to take the offensive and fight Rome. Pyrrhus arrived with a well-trained and battle hardened army of 25,000 men and 24 elephants. He was ready to give battle to the Romans. The Greeks were familiar with the war elephants because of the campaigns of Alexander the Great, where he employed them to devastating effect. In two major battles, Pyrrhus defeated Roman armies, but his forces eventually suffered such heavy losses that he later retired to Sicily. His peace offerings were refused by the Romans and they allied with the Carthaginians, who had also come under attack from Pyrrhus. King Pyrrhus of Epirus returned once more to the mainland in an attempt to conquer the Romans. After being beaten at Beneventum and losing two thirds of his army, he sailed away never to return and left the Tarentines to fend for themselves.

Chapter 2: Carthage and the Punic Wars

It was only a matter of time before Rome and Carthage came into direct conflict with each other. It seemed to be inevitable, especially considering the rise of Rome's power in the Mediterranean. It was ultimately a desire for control of the Straits of Messina that brought them to battle. Italian mercenaries (known as the Mamertines) brought to Sicily by Pyrrhus were in control of the city of Messina. The Mamertines were comprised of several smaller factions. When Sicily was attacked by the Greek city-state of Syracuse, many of those factions appealed to Carthage and Rome for help. This created a situation in which Rome, Carthage, Syracuse, and the Mamertines all became embroiled in conflict.

This led to what became known as the Punic Wars. The First Punic War lasted for 23 years and brought great destruction in the hard-fought conflict. At this time, Rome's armies were comprised of citizen-soldiers. They found success against the mercenary armies employed by Carthage. The war was fought on two fronts, and to win Rome needed to amass naval might. Rome proceeded to construct several fleets. The fleet - combined with new Naval battle tactics - was a force to be reckoned with. Their primary tactic in close range was the practice of coming alongside and boarding the enemy ship. They would throw grapnels aboard the enemy vessel, and well-trained and heavily armed Roman legionaries would slaughter the enemy crew.

The Roman Navy suffered some serious setbacks, despite their victory in 260 at Mylae. The Romans sent an expedition to attack Carthage that turned into a disaster. Despite the Carthaginians being pushed out of Sicily, a decisive result was never achieved. The tide turned when the Roman Navy achieved a victory off of the Aegates Islands. Rome now had command of the seas.

Finally the nations of Rome and Carthage made peace. In the terms of the peace, Carthage gave all Sicilian possessions to the Romans and paid a large sum of money for indemnity. Following the end of the war, Syracuse passed directly to the Romans, who proceeded to organize it as a province. Despite this, Syracuse retained its independence, though it was a client state. The province of Sicily was considered an overseas possession separate from the extensive mainland territories of Rome. Many Imperial administrative measures followed in the next few years, and two magistrates were appointed. One was to take charge of Roman Sicily, and the other was sent to administer to Sardinia in Corsica. This marked the beginning of a Republican Empire.

The Carthaginians themselves responded with great vigor after their concessions at the end of the First Punic War. A new Empire was erected in Spain by Hamilcar Barca, his son-in-law Hasdrubal, and Hamilcar's famous son Hannibal. Hamilcar was bent on exacting revenge on Rome, and Hannibal inherited this mission from him.

    Much remains unknown about Carthage. There is little information about daily life, though some information about the oligarchic city-state constitution that was used has been preserved. These things we do know: the Carthaginian religion partly involved human sacrifices to Baal and other gods. Carthaginian art originated from the Greeks. According to the Romans, Carthage was culturally barren. It is likely that this is nothing more than Roman prejudice against them. What remains of their history and culture is seen primarily through the lens of the Roman victors. Unfortunately, the only Carthaginian book that the Romans felt necessary to translate was an encyclopedia on farming.

In Spain, the Barcas took an aggressive stance that eventually resulted in another war. Both Rome and Carthage seemed eager for a fight and were looking for an opportunity to bring it to pass. An agreement that the Romans and Carthaginians came to into 26 BC recognized Spain south of the river Ebro as Carthaginian territory. The Roman allied city, the city of Saguntum, was on the Spanish south coast of Ebro. Hannibal saw this city as being under Carthaginian control. When he pressed the point, Saguntum refuse to capitulate. In response Hannibal besieged and seized the city. Following this, the Romans declared war. And thus the Second Punic War began.

The most dangerous opponent that the Romans ever faced was arguably Hannibal. He is considered by historians to be one of the greatest generals who has ever lived. His father Hamilcar had instilled within him a hatred of the Roman people, and this led him to focus his great tactical prowess against them. One striking feature of Hannibal is the loyalty he could command in his soldiers. The majority of his men on campaign were mercenaries. They initially fought for money, but ultimately kept fighting out of dedication to the man. His army consisted of a wide array of nationalities, few of whom had any previous commitment to the Carthaginian cause. His army included Numidians, Celts, as well as Spaniards. Hannibal led them to great victories against the Roman legions. The Roman legionaries were citizen-soldiers, raised in a single community, and trained to fight as one united force.

Hannibal soon mastered coordination of his varied troops and forged them into a cohesive and efficient army. Hannibal achieved such great success in large part due to the speed he maintained. Like most great generals throughout history, he understood the importance of keeping the initiative. He changed his tactics frequently and was never afraid to do the unexpected. This supreme tactical skill and leadership became evident during his early campaigns.

The Roman armies confidently invaded Spain and Africa, wielding a tactically superior Navy and a massive reserve of men and equipment. Hannibal demonstrated his initiative by striking first. He headed into Italy and incited the subject city-states of Rome to revolt against their masters. This was effective because it reversed the balance of manpower, spreading the Roman forces thin. Hannibal and his Carthaginian army then marched through Spain and southern France, skillfully avoiding the Roman army. Hannibal soon accomplished his famous feat and crossed the treacherous and snow-covered Alps. Today we have roads and tunnels with which to cross it. Hannibal had only determination, fortitude, and favor of the gods to aid him. It snowed early that year, making the unenviable task of crossing especially difficult. He suffered great losses and by the time he came down into Italy, his force consisted of only

26,000 men, which was half of the original band that he left with. His force of elephants was much depleted, but they would still prove effective and useful in terrorizing the Romans.

Hannibal's reputation grew exponentially after successfully crossing the Alps. His daring maneuver gained him new allies against the Romans. The Celts of the Po Valley joined the Carthaginians to get revenge against the Romans, who had subjugated them a few years previously. Roman forces in Sicily were forced to be recalled just before embarking on their voyage to Africa, in order to repel the Carthaginian invader. They soon joined up with the Roman forces in the north, and combined they attacked Hannibal in December of 218. Hannibal's superior skill led him to victory after he stealthily ambushed and routed the Romans at the battle of Trebia.

An unusually severe winter followed. This gave Rome an opportunity in which to marshal their forces and raise new armies in the war against Carthage. Never one to sit back and wait, Hannibal crossed into central Italy. The Battle of Lake Trasimene followed. When the pursuing Roman army was out-maneuvered and pinned against the lake, Hannibal seemed unstoppable. The Roman army had no way to retreat and was driven into the water, suffering massive casualties. Following this stunning success, Hannibal proceeded into southern Italy. Etruria and Latium both remained loyal to the Romans, and Hannibal needed more allies. In southern Italy he hoped to build alliances and find support among the Samnites and Greeks. The Roman practice of reconciliation made this difficult for the Carthaginians.

The Romans then appointed a dictator known as Fabius Cunctator, or Fabius the Delayer. He was one of their elder statesman. He had apparently been so impressed by Hannibal that he attempted only to buy time to allow Rome to recover. His hopes of wearing down the Carthaginians did not succeed. His policy of passiveness seemed outrageous and laughable to his contemporaries, but it was later considered to have been instrumental in saving Rome. With Rome merely biding its time, Hannibal and his Carthaginian army were free to march through Campania and Apulia. They were allowed to pillage whenever and wherever they wanted. This led to Rome being viewed as impotent by many of their allies. After serving the maximum six-month term as dictator, Fabius was replaced by two new consuls named Paullus and Varro. They immediately rescinded the previous dictator's policies, and raised an army to face the Carthaginians head on. The battle of Cannae followed, and is considered to be one of Hannibal's greatest victories. Conversely, it proved to be an embarrassing and costly Roman disaster.

The Romans were finally determined to defeat Hannibal. In the following campaign year of 216, they mustered a huge army. It was comprised of 87,000 troops – a number that dwarfed the Carthaginian force of around 50,000. The potency of this impressive mobilization was, however, immediately undermined by the election of two consuls who could not deliver the unity that Rome so sorely needed. The two men, Gaius Terentius Varro and Lucius Aemilius Paullus, had wildly divergent views on how the war against Hannibal should be waged. Whereas Paullus favored the old Fabian approach of surrounding Hannibal in his winter quarters and starving him out, Varro was determined to defeat the Carthaginian general in open battle. Even worse, as both consuls went on campaign, each commanded the army on alternate days.

By the end of July, the Roman army had tracked the Carthaginians down to the small Apulian town of Cannae. They set up camp around 10 miles away. On the first of August, after a series of skirmishes, Hannibal marched his troops north across the river Aufidus. There he set up camp and then offered the Romans open battle. Paullus - who was in command that day - pointedly refused to accept the challenge, much to the consternation of his colleague.

The next day - with Varro in command - the Roman army left its main camp on the north bank of the river and crossed to the south. It then drew up in battle formation facing south, with the river to the west. The previous year's consuls, Servilius Geminus and Atilius Regulus (who had replaced the dead Flaminius Nepos), commanded the heavy infantry in the center. Paullus himself led the right wing, where the cavalry and two legions of infantry were situated. Varro then took command of the left wing, made up of 20,000 infantry and some cavalry. Hannibal took time to carefully study the Roman battle line before making a move. Although greatly outnumbered in terms of heavy infantry, he noticed that the Roman infantry in the center were densely packed together. This tight formation would make it difficult for the troops to maneuver.

After crossing the river with his army, he set up a highly unorthodox but tactically brilliant formation. In the center he placed a series of Celtic and Spanish infantry companies in a shallow-stepped line, and at the end of each line he placed his elite and heavily armored Libyan foot soldiers. This left a deliberately weakened center, which he was personally commanding along with his brother Mago. On both right and left wings he placed his cavalry, under the respective commands of his nephew Hanno and the general Hasdrubal. The Roman infantry not only had the sun in their eyes, but also the wind blew up great clouds of dust into their faces. When battle started, however, they predictably quickly drove back the Spanish and Celtic foot soldiers. They soon surged forward into the gap at the center of the Carthaginian formation. Without a moment's pause, they chased after their broken and hastily retreating foe till they took to headlong flight.

They cut their way through the retreating soldiers, who offered no resistance. The Romans reached as far as the Africans who were stationed on both wings, somewhat further back than the Celts and Spaniards who had formed the advanced center. As the latter fell back, the whole front-line became level. As they continued to give ground, it became concave and crescent-shaped, the Africans at either end forming the horns. As the Roman infantry rushed brashly between them, they were encircled by the two wings, which extended and closed round them in the rear.

The Romans were forced to cease pursuing the Celts and Spaniards, whose rear they had been slaughtering. They now commenced a new battle with the African soldiers. It became a very one-sided fight. They were pressured from both sides, and were wearied from the previous fighting. Now they were in combat with fresh and vigorous opponents.

At the same time, the Carthaginian cavalry on the right wing attacked the rear of the Roman right wing. They had already routed the Roman left, and the Romans were now effectively surrounded. After defeating this force, the combined Carthaginian cavalry then attacked the beleaguered Roman infantry from behind. The Romans were now surrounded, and a bloody slaughter quickly ensued. Paullus, who had been seriously wounded by a sling shot, tried to rally his troops. His courageous efforts would soon prove to be in vain. After a while he became too weak to manage his horse, so his cavalry escort dismounted to fight on foot. Although offered the chance to escape on the horse of a fleeing cavalry officer, he refused to leave his men and was eventually killed. Cannae was Rome's greatest military disaster. It is estimated that 70,000 Roman soldiers were killed and another 10,000 captured.

Summary of Cannae

Though the Romans had a numerically superior force, they were decisively defeated. Hannibal employed a clever strategy in which the reinforced center of his formation would be pushed back by the Roman infantry. As the Romans in the center were drawn further into the Carthaginian lines, Hannibal's Celtic horsemen drove off the Roman cavalry. Hannibal then used his African pikemen held in the wings along with his Spaniards to close in from all sides. Thus the Romans were encircled and attacked from the rear. It was a slaughter and the Consul Paullus was killed in the subsequent melee. This marked a turn in the tide of the war. Capua along with several other Italian states declared allegiance to Hannibal. The situation for Rome grew increasingly dire. This was the height of Hannibal's dominance in the war.

The Romans raised additional legions in an effort to swell the ranks, all the while avoiding battle. Eventually they adopted a stance where Roman troops would engage the Carthaginians in battle only when Hannibal was not present. The cities of Syracuse, Capua, and Tarentum were all taken in sieges. Hannibal's brother Hasdrubal was killed soon after. Hannibal's fortunes soon turned for the worse when an equally skilled Roman general named Publius Cornelius Scipio invaded Spain. Scipio managed to drive the Carthaginian army out of the peninsula. By this point Hannibal's manpower was largely depleted. Scipio then invaded Africa and achieved many victories that soon began to threaten Carthage itself. After the 16 years of campaigning in Italy, Hannibal was recalled. The Roman armies were no longer passive and Hannibal could not expect to rampage free. He had finally met his match.

In 206 BC, the battle of Zama took place. Scipio made no amateur mistakes, leaving Hannibal unable to ambush or outflank him. This battle would be a straightforward slugging match between the two armies. The lack of coherence within the Carthaginian army was highlighted from the beginning of the battle, for Hannibal merely exhorted and encouraged his own veterans in the third row, and the responsibility for rousing the other groups fell to the captains. In order to make the initial break through the Roman front line, Hannibal relied on a troop of eighty elephants. However, Scipio had already prepared his force for that particular challenge by creating broad corridors through the three massed ranks of his troops.   When at last the battle began and the elephants charged, most of those beasts that did not panic and rampage back into their own lines were easily channeled down the lanes that cut through the Roman ranks. Taking advantage of the turmoil, Masinissa's horsemen and the Roman cavalry charged their opposite numbers and drove them from the battlefield. Among the infantry, the fight was far more even-handed, with both sides standing their ground and inflicting heavy losses on the other. Eventually the Carthaginian first and second lines were forced back.

After Scipio had reordered his troops into one single massed line, the struggle began against Hannibal's 20,000 battle-hardened veterans, who had been kept in reserve by their commander. The two forces proved evenly matched until the returning Roman cavalry attacked the rear of the Carthaginian lines. More than half of Hannibal's famed soldiers were killed, and those that didn't escape were captured. Zama effectively brought the Second Great War between Rome and Carthage to an end. Hannibal lacked his campaign veterans and unfortunately his Numidian cavalry mercenaries had switched sides. Though he managed to escape, Hannibal's army was destroyed. Carthage proceeded to press for peace negotiations. As part of their terms, they disbanded the Navy, rescinded all claims to Spanish lands, and paid massive war reparations to Rome. Rome additionally gained full control of Sicily because the destruction of Syracuse had eliminated the Greek political power. Because of his great accomplishment in the battle of Zama, Scipio was honored with the title of Africanus. History now remembers him as Scipio Africanus, the general who defeated the Great Hannibal of Carthage.

      Carthage never fully recovered from the war. It was now an ally, albeit a dependent one, of Rome. The general Roman public retained their suspicion of Carthage. Hannibal had focused his efforts on reforming the Carthaginian economy and government after the war, but rumors followed him. He was later accused of plotting to get revenge on the Romans with the Seleuclid Kings of Western Asia. Now pursued, Hannibal was forced to flee. He sought shelter from his enemies and eventually stayed in what is now Turkey. In about 182, his location was betrayed by the king of Bithynia. Hannibal poisoned himself to avoid capture by the

Romans, who undoubtedly had a more painful fate prepared for him.

For the next 30 years Carthage survived unmolested and began to thrive again under the reforms Hannibal had initiated before his death. This prosperity made the Roman government nervous. The paranoia grew to the point where Cato of the Roman Senate finished every speech with the words, "Carthage must be destroyed". Many attempts were deliberately made to provoke the Carthaginians, for once again the Romans were spoiling for a fight. Finally Carthaginian patience waned and they attacked one of Rome's allies.

The Romans proceeded to blockade Carthage for three years beginning in 146. When the blockade ended, they landed and razed the city. The Senate made the decision that no one should ever build again upon those lands and that no crop should ever rise. They destroyed monuments, burned works of art, razed homes to the ground, and took their final revenge by salting the ruined and once fertile lands of Carthage. Roman hatred of the Carthaginians was so complete that they erased nearly all records and evidence of their way of life and achievements.

In Depth

The three long wars waged between Carthage and Rome from 264 to 146 BCE, called the "Punic Wars," pitted the North African maritime trading city-state of Carthage against the power of the militaristic Roman Republic. The conflicts resulted in over a million casualties and a scale of destruction not seen before in the history of warfare. The question remains of who started these wars and for what purpose. Was it the Romans or the Carthaginians? Could it be both?

The Roman Republic is well known for its emphasis on laws and legality. Roman historians present the location of Roman-allied Saguntum on the Tiber river as following the rule of law. Many Roman sources depict their own Empire as one who was always the aggrieved and fought wars only for a just cause: to ward off aggression by others or to defend allies they had agreed to protect. Upon further examination of the historical record, it becomes clearer that all three so-called Punic Wars could likely have been initiated intentionally by Rome under one pretext or another, and not for benevolent or defensive purposes.

At the time of the First Punic War, Sicily was divided between the eastern part, under the control of Syracuse, and the western part, under the influence of Carthage. In 288 BCE, a group known as the Mamertines, renegade Campanian mercenaries, occupied the city of Messina in Sicily. Their first action was killing all the adult males and forcing the women to become their "wives". Defeated in battle by the forces of King Hiero II of Syracuse, the Mamertines secretly called on the Carthaginians and on the Romans for help. The Carthaginians, interested in curtailing Syracusan control, interceded first. They achieved a cessation of hostilities with Hiero and placed a detachment of troops in Messina, the latter to the displeasure of the Mamertines. The Roman Senate, in the meantime - although Rome had no presence or investment in Sicily - voted to send an invasion force to exploit the opportunity to displace the Carthaginians and commence Roman expansion into Sicily. The Roman attack started the First Punic War, which initially saw Carthaginians and Syracusans become allies to try to repel the invaders. After being defeated by the Romans, King Hiero, interested primarily in self-preservation, switched sides. The war then became solely fought between Rome and Carthage.

It soon becomes clear that the Roman invasion was not motivated by altruistic goals. At the same time that Messina was initially occupied by the Mamertines, a similar gang of cutthroat renegade soldiers had taken over Rhegium, right across the narrow strait separating Italy from Sicily. The thugs on the Italian side were severely punished by the Romans and the majority were executed when caught. Consequently, any claim by the Romans that they were interested in the protection of a similar gang in Messina appears false. It becomes clear that expansion and greed were the primary motivators behind the initiation of hostilities that would last 23 years and cost hundreds of thousands of lives.

As for the Second Punic War, pro-Roman historians, such as Polybius and Livy, have tried to blame it on the actions of the famous Carthaginian general, Hannibal Barca. Some believe he was motivated by a need to avenge the wrongs committed against Carthage, as well as fueled by his inherited undying hatred of Rome.

The prelude to the Second War was the Roman annexation of Sardinia, a Carthaginian territory. Carthage at that time was unable to respond due to the devastation caused by the First Punic War and the war it was forced to wage against its own mutinous mercenaries. Hamilcar Barca, Hannibal's father, had been the commander of the Carthaginian land forces in Sicily at the time of the disastrous naval defeat at the Aegates Islands, which compelled Carthage to capitulate in 241 BCE. Although Hamilcar himself remained undefeated in battle, he was forced to accept the defeat of Carthage. He was then put in charge of repatriating the contingents of mercenaries that composed his army. He wisely sent them home gradually, so that they could be paid and dismissed one group at a time. The Carthaginian magistrates misjudged the situation, however. They waited until all the men arrived home and then attempted to negotiate reduced pay. This led to violent mutiny and in the following conflict, characterized by atrocities on both sides, the very survival of the city was at stake. While Hamilcar was able to crush the rebellion, Carthage was exhausted and powerless to resist the theft of Sardinia and later Corsica by the Romans. They later added insult to injury by demanding an additional war reparation under the threat of a new declaration of war.

Hamilcar led an expeditionary force to Spain, to secure the resources that Carthage would need to pay the reparations owed to Rome. For Hamilcar, the last commander of the Carthaginian army in Sicily, the expedition to Spain offered the opportunity not only to be cast as the savior of his homeland, but also to increase the opportunities for autonomous action. Despite his own supporters dominating the Council of Elders and the Popular Assembly, Hamilcar could still expect opposition from the political clique led by his arch-rival, Hanno. For Hanno and his faction it was not foreign adventures but the harnessing of the huge agricultural resources of North Africa which would provide the answer to Carthage's economic woes. The Greek historian Appian reports that Hamilcar defied the wishes of the

Council of Elders when in 237 he set off for Spain.

The Carthaginian elite had traditionally relied on two methods for managing their armies in Sicily. First, they controlled the flow of reinforcements, supplies, and money sent from Carthage. Second, the decisions and actions of their commanders were reviewed at the end of their service, and harsh punishments for mistakes could be meted out. Hamilcar would make sure that there were no such opportunities for scrutinizing his actions in Spain, for he recruited and paid his own troops. Also, Hamilcar never returned to Carthage to answer for his actions, instead relying on partisans in the Council and the Popular Assembly to speak for him. The wealth of Spain was used not only to pay off Carthage's war debts, but also to ensure the support of his army, the Popular Assembly, and his own faction in the Council of Elders. Despite his absence from Carthage, Spanish gold and silver guaranteed Hamilcar's political influence by proxy. In a depressing sign of Carthage's diminished maritime status, the expeditionary force did not have the means to sail directly to Spain, as it would have done in previous times, but marched along the coast of North Africa before making the short crossing at the Pillars of Hercules.

Once Hamilcar arrived in Spain, he could not expect that the task that lay ahead would be an easy one. Carthage had maintained trading relations with the old Phoenician settlements of the Iberian peninsula as well as the Greeks at Ampurias, but it was not certain that Hamilcar and his army would receive a warm welcome. The Iberian and Celtiberian tribes of the interior proved almost uniformly hostile. For Hamilcar, the lack of united political leadership in Spain may have made military campaigning easier, but it made diplomacy far more difficult. He was forced to build a patchwork of individual treaties between each of the different tribal confederations and communities.

Understandably, his priority was to secure control of the all-important gold and silver mines of the Sierra Morena. At the beginning, even the Spanish tribes who had previously cooperated with the Phoenician settlers resisted the Carthaginian advance. In his dealings with the hostile Celtiberian tribes, Hamilcar used much of the experience he gained during the Mercenary Revolt in Carthage. While releasing many of the defeated enemy so that they could return home, he publicly tortured and then crucified one of the chieftains. By carefully juxtaposing clemency with this display of severe punishment, Hamilcar sent out a powerful message to the Spanish tribal leadership of the rewards of cooperation and the consequences of further resistance. This strategy soon bore fruit, as they soon capitulated. Hamilcar quickly commenced a complete reorganization of the mining operation. In contrast to the old Tyrian system, which had left production under indigenous control, a number of mines were taken over by the Barcids. New techniques were brought in from the eastern

Mediterranean to increase efficiency and productivity. Large numbers of slaves performed the manual labor. Underground rivers were redirected through tunnels and shafts, and new technology was used to pump water out of shafts. For the Carthaginians these mining operations were hugely profitable. He was successful in his endeavors, expanding Carthaginian control in Iberia until his death in an ambush in 228, where he sacrificed himself to save the lives of his sons.

Traditionally, the Council of Elders should have selected his successor; however, that precedent had been ignored since the tumultuous events of the Mercenaries' Revolt. Before any decision could be made in Carthage, the army in Spain took matters into their own hands and acclaimed Hasdrubal, Hamilcar's son-in-law, as their new leader. The Popular Assembly then enthusiastically endorsed this decision. Appian relates that tensions were generated when, after he had been appointed commander of the Spanish armies, Hasdrubal returned to Carthage, with the express aim of overthrowing the constitution and introducing his own monarchical rule. After the Council of Elders managed to deny his attempts, Hasdrubal returned to Spain resentfully. He then ruled the Iberian dominions without taking instruction from the Council. Polybius denied the truthfulness of the story on several occasions, but Hasdrubal's previous history of buying public support suggest it is true. Increasingly the standard operating procedure pursued by Hasdrubal in Spain came closely to resemble that of the Hellenistic kingdoms that succeeded the empire of Alexander the Great in the East. In Barcid Spain a small population of foreign elite - backed up by a large mercenary army - ruled over a much larger indigenous population. As in the successor kingdoms, considerable emphasis was placed on the founding of new urban centers and the replenishment of old cities in order to consolidate power over conquered territory and generate much-needed markets and transport hubs. Like Alexander, Hasdrubal attempted to make himself more acceptable to the indigenous population by marrying the daughter of a local king. Hasdrubal continued Carthaginian expansion, mostly by diplomatic means, until he was killed in 221.

It was during his rule that the Romans, concerned with the success of the Carthaginians, sent a delegation to establish the Ebro Treaty. By it, the Carthaginians agreed to accept the boundary of the river Ebro. They were not permitted to cross in strength of arms. Interestingly enough, the Roman historians do not inform us about Rome's responsibilities under the treaty, although obviously there must have been some equally beneficial term made: Rome was not to interfere south of the Ebro.

The Romans implicitly violated the Ebro treaty by forming an alliance with the city of Saguntum, which was south of the Ebro and thus within Carthaginian territory. There is no evidence that such an alliance existed prior to the signing of the treaty. Not only that, but Rome encouraged the Saguntines to massacre Carthaginian partisans in their city and to commit aggressive actions against the Turboleti, a tribe under Carthaginian protection. By this point, Hannibal had already been voted by acclamation the new commander-in-chief of the Carthaginian forces in Spain. He reacted by marching against Saguntum and taking it by storm, after an eight-month-long siege. During those eight months the Saguntines sent repeated requests for assistance to Rome, to no avail—no help materialized. The Romans waited until Saguntum had fallen and then sent a delegation to Carthage to demand that Hannibal be turned over to them for punishment. Following the refusal of the Carthaginian assembly, Rome declared war on Carthage.

The Romans were confident of victory. Since they now controlled the Mediterranean, they were not concerned with an attack on Italy from the sea. Since the supposedly impassable natural barrier of the Alps in the north protected them from an invasion by land, they expected to wage the new war in Spain and in North Africa, the land of their enemies. Consequently, they sent an army to the south, under the consul Sempronius Longus. He was to cross over to Africa from Sicily. They sent another army west, under consul Publius Cornelius Scipio the Elder, to invade Spain. They would soon find themselves outmatched by the military genius of Hannibal. It is clear however that the Romans themselves played a decisive role in instigating the Second Punic War.

The Third Punic War was waged against a Carthage that no longer posed any threat to Rome, 34 years after the death of Hannibal. It was motivated by the hatred exemplified in the phrase "Carthage must be destroyed!" that ended every talk of the bitter Roman senator and moralist, Cato the Elder. Many in Rome were also jealous of the African city's economic recovery following its defeat in the Second Punic

War. Hannibal's work as magistrate after the war had served to eliminate corruption in their government and had allowed Carthage to offer to pay off the crippling reparations imposed by Rome much faster than expected.

Another condition imposed on Carthage at the end of the Second Punic War proved fatal—a prohibition to wage war, even in self-defense, without permission from Rome. The Romans encouraged the aggression of the Numidian king, Masinissa, who kept encroaching on Carthaginian territory. Appeals from Carthage for Rome to intervene were ignored. When finally the Carthaginians attempted to defend themselves, Rome used this as excuse to declare war. The Carthaginians did not want war, and offered capitulation plus the payment of further reparations. The Romans demanded that in addition they also provide hostages and surrender all weapons in the city. Once the Carthaginians had complied, the Romans revealed their true intentions. They demanded that the entire population leave the city, moving south into hostile territory where their survival would be practically impossible, and declared that Carthage would be destroyed. The Carthaginians understandably refused this and proceeded to heroically defend their city against a Roman siege for three long years. When the Romans finally breached the city's defenses, they engaged in a frenzy of wholesale slaughter, what we would call today ethnic cleansing or genocide. The great city was razed and burned to the ground. The inhabitants—men, women, and children—were slaughtered, and the survivors were sold into slavery. The libraries and records of the defeated were destroyed in the process, leaving only pro-Roman accounts to tell the story. It was a true holocaust that resulted in over 700,000 Carthaginian deaths, the first total genocide in recorded history. It was the murder and extermination of an entire people and the erasure of their culture.

The causes of war - of any war - tend to be complex, and include social, cultural, economic, and psychological factors. The Punic Wars were no exception.

The instigators of the wars between Rome and Carthage appear to be primarily the Romans. It can be inferred that their primary motivations were greed, hatred, and a thirst for conquest. The ultimate defeat of Carthage opened the gates for the legions of Rome to march and conquer as they pleased in the Mediterranean world. The expansionist Roman Empire had been born.

Rome's victory was complete and they now controlled the entirety of the Western Mediterranean. Immediately efforts began to organize the new territory and create domestic reforms. The focus of Rome had shifted and they were reluctant to get involved with foreign affairs. However, enmity still remained toward Philip V of Macedon for his support of Hannibal in the Second Punic War. Situated in the Eastern

Mediterranean, Macedon was a great power along with the Seleucid Empire and Ptolemaic Egypt. When the Greco-Macedonian empire of Alexander had broken down following his death, the three dynasties established themselves. The entire region was filled with powerful cities and great wealth. Each was fundamentally and politically Greek and could be described as Hellenistic.

Chapter 3: Vacuum of Power

Roman involvement was bound to occur, and eventually these great powers came to a head. Philip V began his conquest of Rhodes and other Greek city-states. Before long these Greek city-states asked Rome for help. In 197, the Roman intervention resulted in a decisive victory against the Macedonians. As terms of their defeat, Macedon was stripped of the land Philip had taken. Rome also claimed the Macedonian fleet and gold as war reparations. After liberating the Greek city-states, Rome withdrew their military.

The Seleucid king Antiochus saw his opportunity. Attempting to fill the power vacuum, he invaded Greece. The Romans returned and proceeded to defeat him at Thermopylae in 191 and drove his forces from the Greek lands. The Greeks continued to squabble amongst themselves. Rome completely destroyed the historic city of Corinth in 146 to sufficiently humble the Greeks. The Seleucids fought another war against Macedon when Macedon and the Greek states joined Rome. 13 years later the leader of Pergamum died and passed his lands and resources on to his Roman allies. The growth of the Roman Empire was massive and by this point placed a terrible strain on their political system. This growth has occurred within a few short generations, and the Roman way of life began to suffer. Rome had grown fat on the profit of their successes and conquest. Citizens grew into even greater luxury, laws became more lax, and the youngest generation became difficult to control. The priorities of their culture had shifted. In a twist of irony – despite and because of the Roman conquest of Greece – Greek literature, philosophy, and arts ingrained themselves in the cultural norm of Rome. Roman citizens bought large quantities of Greek statues and paintings, and as most starving artists would resort, the Greeks would willingly sell.

There was a conservative group among the Romans who were bothered by this new sophistication and believed it incompatible with the basic Roman virtues that founded their republic. They believed that luxury bred softness and that this arrogance was counter to the example of former dictator Cincinnatus, who wanted nothing more than to defend his home. The old Roman system had begun to break down, and the Senate was now controlled solely by powerful aristocrats. Many capitalists and businessmen resented their exclusion from the Roman political system. The tenement blocks of Rome ran wild with landless and homeless people. It had become a world where peasants and regular citizens could not compete against slave labor. Others grew restless when Italian cities - now part of the Roman empire - did not receive the privileges and rights of Roman citizenship. Distrust grew in many of the new provinces of the Roman empire when they believed that they were being cheated by their governors and tax collectors. The Roman administration had grown exponentially, but was still only prepared and designed to govern in a city-state rather than an empire.

The astonishing thing about Rome is that despite all of the Civil Wars and conflicts that erupted, it managed to endure and survive. Rome was often engaged in multiple conflicts with foreign enemies, as well as domestic crises. One such crisis occurred when the Tribune Gracchus proposed a series of drastic reforms in an effort to re-create a class of farmers. This reform would have reduced the size of the estates and used that surplus to fund it. The conservative body of the Senate opposed the measure, so in an effort to pass this reform he persuaded the Assembly of the People. The conservatives of the convention were incensed because in their eyes this violated the conventions of their constitution. When Tiberius Gracchus later sought reelection, a group of senators - aided by their followers - assassinated him in the capitol. The real reasons for the murder and the outcome they hoped for are unknown, perhaps acting out of self-interest or genuine fear of what was to come. Most interestingly, this was the first recorded act of serious violence in the Roman political sphere. Ultimately it would foreshadow the slaughter that would follow in years to come. Approximately 10 years later Tiberius' younger brother Gaius was elected to the same position as Tribune and he continued his brothers program, only this time taking an even more radical stance. He proposed redistribution of the land as well as measures to help keep the price of wheat low. He established a program of public works to fight unemployment, and also established new colonies in Italy and abroad. Because these measures were designed to help the poor, they were easily passed by the Assembly of the People. The Senate once again disapproved. Gaius fairly proposed to extend Roman citizenship to the Latin peoples and give their other Italian allies the same rights that they were due. This time however, the Assembly of the

People was not swayed or persuaded because they did not want to share their privileges. Gaius then failed to be reelected and soon the Senate issued an emergency decree giving the consuls the authority to take whatever actions and use any measures to 'save the Roman state'. The consuls proceeded to use this power to massacre any supporters of Gaius. He himself committed suicide to avoid being captured.

    This is a distinctive point where we can clearly see that Roman politics had shifted on both sides to become more of a matter of personal gain and ambition. Many politicians used their positions for the benefit of themselves and their friends rather than the patriotic conviction that had defined the early history of Rome. Roman politics soon divided into personal parties and political machines that were funded by powerful families, and they would attempt to discredit and destroy each other. For approximately 10 years after the death of Gaius, the ruling elite remained unchallenged. The war against the Numidians weakened their position, however, with the way it was incompetently handled. Command of the army was finally given to Marius, an officer of humble birth. The Senate disapproved. He immediately set to creating a new type of paid professional Roman army which proved to be more loyal to its leaders than to the state itself. The Numidian leader Jugurtha was finally defeated and captured after the negotiations conducted by Lucius Cornelius Sulla, Marius's Lieutenant. Jugurtha was then executed.

Marius went on to win a series of victories against the Germanic tribes who had shocked the Roman world when they invaded Italy. Marius wielded great power within the state, but even more important were the veteran soldiers that he had obtained land grants for. After making clumsy political mistakes as consul, he retired.

Violence broke out once more in 91 BC. Another Tribune – named Drusus – was murdered for his politically progressive views.

He had also proposed giving rights to the Italians and Latins and other allies of Rome. The Italians by this point were so incredibly frustrated that they reacted violently to the disappointment of their hopes. They raised an army in revolution, proclaimed a new Italian Republic, and fought with such effective ferocity that Rome only claimed the victory by conceding citizenship to all Italians who would throw down their arms and cease fighting. This effectively resulted in all free Italians becoming Roman citizens with all of the rights and privileges afforded to that position.

Sulla had demonstrated his military talents in this war against the Italians, and soon proved to be the rival of his former commander Marius. He came from an aristocratic background and was careful to not make the same mistakes in the assembly and Senate that his mentor had. In 88 BC Sulla was given command of the Army and led it in battle against Mithrdates VI of Pontus, who had found success invading Roman Asia due to the disillusionment of the population. Marius - who had returned from retirement - took command of the Army himself and allied with the Tribune Sulpicius. The plebeian assembly then named him officially to replace Sulla at the head of the Army. Instead of relinquishing his command to his former mentor, Sulla marched on Rome. He occupied the Roman Capitol, had Tribune Sulpicius executed, and negated the Plebeian Assembly's decision. Sulla was the conservative champion of Rome, firm in his desires to restore Rome to the old ways. Yet he showed a distinct lack of respect for the Constitution of the state. Sulla then left Rome and marched out to deal with Mithridates. Marius had previously fled to Africa but then returned to Rome, allying himself with the consul Cornelius Cinna. Finding himself once again in control of the Capitol, he exacted his revenge upon all who had stood against him. Before Marius could follow and engage Sulla in battle, he died at about 70 years old.

Sulla then defeated Mithridates and turned his attention toward Roman Asia. He proceeded to loot the cities, invade Italy, and destroy the Marians. Marius was now the master of the Roman state. Sulla then had himself declared dictator in a fraudulent attempt to 'restore the state'. The dictatorship had been legally abolished over a century previously, and this new variation that Sulla brought back did not include the liberty-preserving limitation of only six months in holding that office.

Using his newly minted power, Sulla conducted campaigns of terror on Roman soil, killing everyone who opposed him. He instructed his men to post lists in public places of those he declared outlaws, and they were to be killed on sight. He enacted a series of reforms that seemed counter to his actions. His reforms made the Senate more representative, made the Tribune's less powerful, and protected the state against ambitious generals like himself. Within 10 years of his death in 79, most of his enactments were rescinded. What Sulla failed to realize was that his violence against the state – even with the intention of reforming it – would destroy instead of preserving those traditions.

In Depth

Sulla emerged as a significant player in Roman politics during a conflict between Rome and her Italian allies, referred to as the "Social War". He captured many enemy cities by conquest throughout the war and attained a reputation as a formidable military commander. Sulla campaigned for the Consulship in 88 BC and was elected nearly unanimously. At this time, a varied combination of foreign and domestic conflicts caused a full-blown civil war. First, King Mithridates VI of Pontus invaded and conquered the Roman province of Asia. Mithridates's intrusion was a significant blow to Roman prestige and posed a credible threat. It absolutely was made all the worse since most people of Asia - angered by Roman exploitation - planned to defect over to Mithridates. This decision soon proved catastrophically disastrous and a massacre of Roman citizens in Asia took place. In this massacre, as large a number as 80,000 Roman citizens perished. Despite this, the Romans anticipated to be able to beat Mithridates with a fairly minimal effort. The only question remaining was whom should be appointed to command the expedition to expel them. The main contenders were the now elderly Marius and his former protege Sulla.

The competition was intense because the appointment to this position was of immense prestige. It would bring not only glory, but significant riches gained from the spoils of war, along with added political weight. A victorious return would undoubtedly ensure considerable power in the Roman capitol. The Senate appointed the great burden of responsibility upon Sulla, but Marius's influence was still sufficient enough to persuade the Roman Senate to pass the Command position on to him. Then when Marius sent two officers to relieve Sulla of his command, those officers were promptly killed by Sulla's men. Marius himself had used the Roman army for Roman political gain, and unfortunately his rival used a similar tactic.

Sulla had the distinction of being the first Roman leader to march his army on Rome, but in time proved to not be the last. He soon expelled the supporters of Marius from the city by force. Having now secured his command from all domestic opposition, Sulla left Italy for Greece and Asia. Marius soon came back, ended up being elected Consul, and later passed away in 86 BC. Even with Marius dead, the stage was set for a civil war. The feud between the factions of the senate had yet to be resolved. When the feud finally came to a head, Sulla traveled to Rome to secure his Senatorial support. Meanwhile, Marius's successor Cinna sought to gain the support of the people. Cinna's followers were able to intimidate the Senate. They seized control from the Popular Assembly and declared Sulla an outlaw.

In Greece, Sulla declared himself the supreme dictator in place of the Roman government. This crisis at home would soon take a violent turn. In the meantime, Sulla turned his attentions to the continuing war in Asia. Sulla proved himself an effective and surprisingly merciful leader. As he laid siege to Athens, the Athenians sent out a diplomat to attempt to persuade Sulla to be merciful. He then proceeded to drive the forces of Mithridates out of Greece with great haste, and finally he signed a peace treaty. In 83 BC. Sulla landed in Italy and marched on Rome again. Together with his legions approaching Rome, more and more senators abruptly began to open their eyes and see the threat of Sulla.

Sulla defeated the troops sent to oppose him at the Colline gate of Rome and entered the city. Sulla ordered the Senate brought to see him at the Temple of Mars.

He then proceeded to speak to the frightened senators over the tumult. Sulla had ordered the 6,000 Roman soldiers he captured en route to Rome to be executed inside the Circus Maximus. The senators were dumbfounded by his barbarity. Sulla remained relaxed and unmoved by the screams from the massacre unfolding elsewhere in the city. With this horrifying backdrop, the Senate was easily coerced to grant him dictatorial powers for "writing laws and regulations." More astonishing and horrifying was his unexpected bloodthirsty interest in vengeance on his enemies.

Most people had likely anticipated a few dozen executions of his many public opponents, but Sulla, took this a terrifying step further. His first step would be to simply try to eliminate the opposition. He posted lists of names of men whom were "proscribed" as enemies of the state. Proscribed individuals might be killed on sight, and those who carried out the state sanctioned killings were rewarded by that state. Their property was then seized and Sulla used it reward his soldiers. As many as 10,000 slaves received their freedom from Sulla for murdering their masters. When the killing showed no indication of ending, the Senate appealed to him. It didn't wish to plead for mercy for those whom he meant to destroy, but merely requested that he at least declare all who he saw fit to spare. Sulla took this recommendation literally and started posting lists of every single individual proscribed. Forty senators, 1,600 veteran officers, and several of their supporters were proscribed. It has been estimated that as many 100,000 Roman citizens fell target to Sulla's purge and the violence surrounding it.

The origins and true motivations behind Sulla's purge remain unknown even today. Plutarch among others found his behavior terrifying in how erratic it was. Nevertheless, there were particular social groups in Roman culture that received the dictator's wrath in unique and heavy measure. Sulla's hatred was directed especially at the rich businessmen and politicians that had succeeded in acquiring great wealth and social status to which he believed they were not entitled. Sulla wished finally to restore the authority of the patricians and also the senate, even when that meant the murder of numerous senators. Sulla additionally struck at the leaders of the popular party.

Young Julius Caesar belonged to the social circle of Sulla's victims. As Marius's nephew and Cinna's son-in-law, Julius Caesar ended up growing to become a man of some significant importance despite the fact that he had been only 18 years of age. Caesar was subsequently forced into hiding for fear of his life for several weeks. Finally, he was then brought before Sulla. A number of influential Romans pleaded with Sulla for Caesar's life. He was spared, but only barely.

Yet Sulla remains in history as more than just a mass murderer. When he was later asked why he marched upon the capitol of Rome with his full military might, he responded, "To free it from tyrants." He thought that Rome's greatest problems had been the weakening of the Senate's authority, combined with the considerable measure of power wielded by the Tribunes of the Plebs, as well as rebellious armed forces commanders (like himself).

He utilized his place as dictator to try and turn back the clock to the 5th Century. The Senate's legislative veto power was then subsequently restored. The office of Tribune of the People had its veto power removed. It was also limited by law to one year in office, and those in that office were forbidden to ever hold any political position beyond tribune. His objective was to reaffirm the governmental privileges of the Senate and curtail the effectiveness of the Tribunes.

Using all of the legal and illegal means offered to him, Sulla made every attempt possible to restore a regular senatorial regime which could work and govern effectively. He doubled the size of the senate, therefore broadening the governing class. Of course, the new members had been very carefully selected. If his objective would be to strengthen Senatorial authority, the means he selected to accomplish those objectives could not attain this goal. The means included army coups, proscriptions, essentially legalized murder, and dictatorial reforms enforced at sword-point.

    Above all, Sulla could perhaps not cancel the effect of his march on Rome. Men like Sulla had risen to the very upper echelons of power by violence rather than merit; they needed armies to fight against their political opponents rather than settling their disputes amicably. He spent large amounts of money securing the support of veteran soldiers. After purchasing their support in this way, he failed to realize that he had made his entire country something that could be bought on the market. They had placed themselves in a position where they had to be slaves of the worst type of people in order to be the masters of the better. He had seized absolute power in title for the patricians but barely used their assistance. His armies had become the problem, all while the nobles had looked on helplessly.

Despite his constitutional reforms and the semi-legal basis of his dictatorship, the truth ended up being that his power rested upon his 120,000 veteran soldiers. It was a completely futile effort. Rome could not forget four centuries of political development and Sulla simply ignored that. Sulla may have made himself the permanent ruler of Rome, but he saw himself as the republic's savior, not its enemy.

In 79 BC he declared his work complete and retired from public affairs and returned to his life of pleasure. A year after retirement, he passed away. Julius Caesar later commented that Sulla had neglected to master the rudiments of politics and went on to say that he was a fool to stop the dictatorship.

Sulla's bloody purge had the effect of setting a dangerous precedent in Rome. Instead of trying to resolve struggles peacefully, force was now the answer to problems that could not be quickly solved. His reforms tried to put Roman politics in a noose, but he could not undo the effect of his own position. Especially after over-utilizing the army and using them to march on Rome and overthrow the government in the name of reform. Within a few years of his death, other generals would follow his example. Even more troubling was the example Sulla had set together with his bloody proscriptions of his enemies. His actions had escalated civil disagreements to civil war. His actions have puzzled ancient authors and modern scholars alike, for he had been a series of contradictions: bloodthirsty yet generous, a tyrant who murdered in the name of the Senate. The most perplexed was Julius Caesar. Caesar grew to become an autocrat focused on imposing his own rule in the Roman world, whereas Sulla finally saw himself as a defender of an aristocratic class. His reforms can be seen as an attempt to halt the drift towards tyranny by showing the Romans just how terrifying a tyrant can be. Sulla's biggest and most lasting contribution to Roman history was a negative one: he demonstrated how a commander could turn his army into a massive body of loyal power and make use of them to achieve his supreme goals. Everyone who later utilized armed forces to seize power in Rome thereafter was in a sense following in his footsteps.

Chapter 4: The Triumvirate

By this point of Roman history it had become evident that the old order was incapable of managing such a largely expanded empire, as well as coping with the political and domestic problems on the home front. The Roman state continued to depend more heavily upon their military leaders. The laws that Sulla had enacted were under attack. Many attempts were made to reverse his edicts and restore power to the Tribunes. None of these attempts were successful until the arrival of a young Roman general named Pompey, who had previously been one of Sulla's lieutenants. He and Marcus Licinius Crassus would be the ones responsible for sweeping away Sulla's constitution. The Senate was very suspicious of successful soldiers because of the events in the recent past of Rome, and this initially restricted their influence. This in turn encouraged them to circumvent the

Senate in ways that would ultimately destroy the Republic.

Crassus and Pompey found themselves working together to achieve their political ambitions, despite the fact that they were rivals. Crassus had exploited his previous positions to become rich and through smart investments became extraordinarily wealthy and well-connected. His reputation achieved in the military was not as great as Pompey's, but his services were equally as valuable. Crassus was charged with defeating the forces led by Spartacus, a Thracian who had rebelled from a gladiator school at Capua and formed an army of runaway slaves. These former slaves and gladiators plundered Italy and battled against the Roman armies for three years from 73 to 71 BC before being trapped in southern Italy by Crassus's troops. The army was destroyed and all prisoners were crucified along the Appian Way, spanning all the way to Capua where it began.

Pompey had achieved a wider range of victories in his military career. As a young man he fought in Africa, and because of his great victories he was awarded by Sulla with the title of Pompeius Magnus, meaning 'Pompey the Great'. Furthermore, he fought in Spain and returned to Italy in time to help Crassus mop up the war against Spartacus. Interestingly, the two generals did not turn against each other and instead helped one another reach greater political heights. Using their joint efforts they both became consuls in the year 70 BC. After taking office, the two of them set immediately to restoring the power of the tribunes as well as removing the Senate's sole power over the court laws.

When his year of service as consul had ended, Pompey retired into private life. It does not appear that he had any concrete political aims, but would continue to serve Rome whenever the opportunity arose. Crassus did not fare as well. He had less opportunities to see action and tried unsuccessfully to build his political career. Then in 67 BC Pompey received a special commission to eliminate the Pirates in the Mediterranean who had been sacking cities and threatening grain shipments and other supplies to Rome. In only three months, Pompey accomplished his mission and drove the Pirates from one stronghold to another until he completely destroyed their power. The next year he engaged in another campaign, this time against Mithridates VI of Pontus. He was also responsible for the official incorporation of Syria into the Empire. He arrived back in Rome in 62 BC at the age of only 42 years old. Upon returning to the capitol, he disbanded his army to the surprise of many.

Roman politics were growing increasingly complicated. Two of the most influential figures in Rome at this point were Cato, great-grandson of the same Cato who called for the destruction of Carthage, and Cicero. Cicero was more moderate than Cato and was considered to be an excellent orator. Cicero's main political goal was to unite the Senate in the ideal that law and order are more important than the desires of any single individual. When Cicero was elected consul in 63 BC, his defeated opponent Catiline began plotting against him. Although lacking definite proof, Cicero criticized him so severely and effectively during a Senate meeting that all who sat near Catiline moved away, and finally he was left in guilty isolation. A short time later Catiline fled Rome and joined his supporters in Etruria. After Cicero persuaded the Senate to round up and execute his co-conspirators, Catiline was killed in battle. Many in Rome celebrated Cicero as a hero.

    Another rising political force in Rome was Gaius Julius Caesar. He had narrowly escaped execution by Sulla due to his family connections with Marius. For a period of time early in his career, Caesar and Crassus worked together. Crassus's money helped finance Caesar's rising political ambitions. Pompey returned from the

East and formed an alliance alongside Crassus and Caesar. This alliance was a powerful combination with political, military, and financial strengths and is referred to as the First Triumvirate. Caesar himself became a consul in 59 BC and held a five-year command of Roman provinces on both sides of the Alps.

Julius Caesar's quest for power was only just beginning. He surprised many back in Rome when his prodigious military skill came to light. Capitalizing on his own ambitions, he conquered Gaul all the way from the Atlantic to the Rhine. This added vast new lands and riches to the Roman Empire. The alliance between Pompey and Crassus began to break down and showed signs of strain. Caesar held a conference and proposed to them both that new arrangements be made. Then in 55 BC , one was given a command in Spain and the other was given command in the East. Caesar himself extended his commission for five additional years. Within the next two years Caesar bridged the Rhine and invaded the great forests of Germany. He was also the first to cross the English Channel and fight the Celts deep in Britain. Finally the Gauls were able to ally their tribes together against Caesar. Led by Vercingetorix, the attacks carried out against Caesar stretched his resources and skills to the breaking point. But when Vercingetorix was captured at Alesia in 52 BC, the last pockets of resistance were broken.

In Depth

The creation of the the "First Triumvirate" by Gaius Julius Caesar, Gnaius Pompeius Magnus, and Marcus Licinius Crassus definitely stands among the many crucial occasions in Roman Republican history. Ironically, its inception and the ensuing power swing that it created, ended up being the beginning of the end for that very republic. While these men had weaknesses while separate, together they were almost untouchable. The optimates that sought to lessen the influence of the Triumvirate proved unsuccessful. The alliance seemed, at the least at the start, to be the right combination for managing Roman politics. Ultimately however the personalities of the three led them in various directions and conflicts. While the destruction of the Triumvirate is frequently ascribed to the deaths of Crassus and Julia(Caesar's sister), this might be an overly simplistic explanation. To understand the reasons for the rift, one must first understand the men who comprised the alliance.

It brought together three effective and powerful men who all wanted to be in ultimate control of Rome. Pompey was the decorated hero from Rome's past. Caesar was to be Rome's hero in the future. But ultimately both desired to be the lauded Roman hero in the present. Crassus was the man whose own significant achievements had been overshadowed by both. His drive to surpass Pompey was his undoing, as he was given an ignoble death in the middle of a catastrophic defeat.

The alliance among them was thus doomed from the beginning, with three men competing for the same position: to be the most powerful man in Rome. Caesar proved to be the most cunning, as Pompey was far too susceptible to believe the flattery constantly heaped upon him by those who would try to sway him for their ambitions. Specifically, the optimates who vehemently hated Caesar. To Caesar, the Triumvirate was an instrument to be used, and he quickly became a master at utilizing it.

The literal definition of a Triumvirate is a small grouping of three ruling with equal power. When it comes to the popularly named "First Triumvirate", this isn't entirely accurate. The three politicians in question never ruled during the Triumvirate. In addition, the partnership - especially toward the end - was far from equal.

Caesar's daughter Julia then became his rival Pompey's spouse. The civil war that forced the men's split was regrettable, but was simply the final part of Caesar's plan for the Republic. The success of the Triumvirate, at least at first, ended up being based on a shared need for help among the three. For one, the money of Crassus and Pompey. By 60 BC they were the two richest politicians in Rome, accomplished by frequently "greasing the gears of state". There were few things or people that both of these men could perhaps not buy, and their money was utilized extensively in the effort of securing friendly Tribunes along with other magistrates throughout their alliance. The money later ended up being lavishly invested to secure the Consular elections of Caesar and Pompey.

While Caesar did not contribute a great deal of cash to the cause, what he did bring was a respected and noble family name. This was combined with a formidable political presence that gained the support of the Popular Party with supreme ease. Particularly in its very earliest incarnation, the alliance among these three was seen by contemporaries to be dominated by Pompey, not Caesar, though he would get to be the dominant figure among later historians. Certainly Pompey and Caesar were the key members of the three, with the aging Crassus later becoming the "third wheel".

Though there is some disagreement as to whether Caesar formally allied himself to Pompey and Crassus before or after his very first election towards the Consulship, it is not debated that he definitely used a substantial amount of bribery to secure that election.

Life of Pompey in Detail

Gnaius Pompeius Magnus was a noted legend in his own time, and even more so in his own head. During his popularity in Roman politics, he made his mark as both a competent general and an excellent administrator. As a new leader he took it upon himself to levy troops in support of Sulla during the civil wars. He had been merely 23 at that time, but this motion on his part catapulted him to the forefront of Roman politics. He served for several more years under Sulla, and accounted for himself quite well in actions in Africa and Spain against the Marians. His success garnered him high praise from Sulla, who revealed to Pompey respect that he scarcely ever revealed to older, more experienced commanders.

After his successes in Africa, Pompey, who had yet to even enter the Senate, was given proconsular imperium and ended up being provided the task of taking on Sertorius in Spain. These early actions were pivotal in creating the man that Pompey would become in his older age. One incident in particular - that of the slave rebellion of Spartacus in 73 BC - was terribly important to later affairs, primarily since it proved to be the beginning of the long-lasting animosity between Pompey and Crassus. After several consular armies had been defeated in Italy, the panic within the Senate caused them to send Pompey to subdue the threat. As opportunity would have it, an army commanded by Crassus actually defeated the rebellion while Pompey was still on his way. A small group of slaves did manage escape to the North. Pompey encountered this remnant group and promptly defeated them, claiming credit for putting down Spartacus.

Crassus later resented Pompey for stealing his moment of glory, a fact which put considerable stress on their working relationship. Given the immense amount of success Pompey enjoyed at such an early age, it is perhaps forgivable that he started to develop what would one day become a truly monumental ego. It is ironic that the very self-confidence - born in no small part by his ignorance of defeat - that propelled him to the top, also was responsible for his downfall against Caesar decades later. Pompey served as consul with Crassus in the year 70 BC, after which he took time away from public politics to "sleep on his laurels", though perhaps not wholeheartedly. He had been all too mindful of the troubles brewing within the east, and for the most part waited for the proper moment to again appear as the hero. That moment came as he was called as the man to curtail the Mediterranean pirates, which for generations had been wreaking havoc on shipping. This command was an astounding success, and at this moment Pompey's great skill at company command and management came to light.

Permitted to choose his own legates, Pompey divided the sea into thirteen zones, assigning subordinates with ships and troops in every single area. His ability to choose capable commanders proved to be a tremendous benefit, and within three months the pirate threat was eliminated. With more than two years still remaining in his imperium, Pompey then moved East. Securing an extension to his currently unprecedented command, Pompey struggled against the rebelling monarchs Mithridates VI of Pontus and Tigranes of Armenia in 66 BC.

Over the next three years Pompey defeated a succession of outmatched Eastern Monarchs until nearly all of the East, from Armenia to Jerusalem, ended up being under Roman control. In 62 BC Pompey returned to

Italy, his reputation and legacy secure. After all, he had single-handedly conquered both the pirates as well as the East, securing a more glorious future for Rome. While Pompey's accomplishments had been no doubt impressive, he had essentially succeeded against a collection of criminals and has-been rulers with diminished power. His victories appeared even more impressive due to the complete mediocrity of the predecessors who had previously faced them. This is not to say that Pompey did not possess greater abilities or influence. The ease of his victories certainly denoted a great deal of ability, but also proved to be dangerous for his future. Pompey had yet to experience defeat, and the resulting air of invulnerability would not last forever.

During Pompey's years away, Julius Caesar was making a name for himself in Roman politics. Though he had not yet amassed power or influence to rival Pompey, he had been quickly gaining support. While Pompey was the high-regarded and conquering hero, Caesar was somewhat of a dark horse: the enigma. Although the product of a noble and proud household, Gaius Julius Caesar did not rise with a simple path to governmental success. The Julians, though aristocrats, were historically unsuccessful in politics. They were therefore not respected in practical terms and success by the other patricians. Caesar did however have the advantage of being the nephew of Gaius Marius, whose proud tradition Caesar would find himself following later on in life.

Plutarch mentions that, when Sulla was being convinced that Caesar was not worth killing, he (Sulla) remarked that within Caesar he saw the equal of "many of Marius". This could be the product of exaggeration on Plutarch's part, but the point remains that even early in life many believed Caesar would grow to be great. It was that same great reputation that saw him safely through abduction by pirates on his way to Rhodes years later.

Life of Caesar in Detail

Throughout the 70 BCs, Caesar began to rise to the forefront of the Roman political arena. This was aided in part by the accusations raised against the proconsul Dolabella in letters sent to Rome. In that particular case, he accused the returning proconsul of extortion in his former province of Macedonia. Though Dolabella was acquitted, the attempt gained Caesar great popularity and appeal in Rome, and served as a sizable boost to his political career. Throughout his climb up the social and governmental ladder, Caesar exhibited a remarkable arrogance in relation to the world around him. He had been known to invest enormous amounts of money on luxurious events, villas in the countryside, art, and slaves. At all times he displayed an easy nonchalance for all to see, even though it had been stated that his debts were reaching eight million denarii. Caesar was no simple playboy, however. Despite what his opponents or other contemporaries might have thought, it had been all part of his master plan. He knew that in order to break into the uppermost echelon of Roman politics, one must acquire powerful allies. Such friends were costly to secure.

Furthermore, Caesar also had to look the part to achieve the widespread political acceptance he needed. Caesar was all too aware of these necessary components of his success. He therefore embarked on an all-or-nothing gamble: he racked up massive amounts of financial obligations in the understanding that he would be able to achieve success and pay them back tenfold. It was this ambition combined with his considerable cunning, that made him so capable and dangerous. In 69 BC, Caesar attained the position of quaestor, and with it he gained membership in the Senate. From there he served in Spain briefly, accompanied by a stint in Gaul. He proved himself to be an ardent supporter of granting full citizenship and rights to those living in these provinces. Though his efforts were unsuccessful, he did gain further support from the common people there, which successfully aided him in his future endeavors. In 66 BC, Caesar announced his complete support of the bill providing Pompey the power to declare war and grant aid on behalf of Rome. This he hoped would serve to garner favor from Pompey himself. Though Pompey was a Sullan in days past, Caesar knew the need for powerful allies, and there were none at that time that had anything near the power that Pompey wielded.

The year of 66 BC saw Caesar's election as an aedile, a post which emphasized the investing of yet more income on general public games and festivals. Caesar did this without hesitation, and this increased his popular opinion while simultaneously increasing his already substantial debts. The next few years saw Caesar further embroiled in domestic politics. This also marked his very first association with Crassus. The two became connected in the minds of the people primarily because they both saw and took advantage of governmental opportunities that stemmed from the great unrest of the times.

It is at this point that Caesar came into his own at the forefront of Roman politics. In the year 63 BC he was elected as the high priest of Rome, a prestigious position in itself. He followed this up by winning the election to the praetorship in the next year. The board was set and the pieces positioned for the Triumvirate to rise.

Life of Crassus in Detail

Crassus is the least well-known of the three in modern culture. Despite this, he played an important part in the foundation and success of the Triumvirate. Older than both Pompey and Caesar by nine to fifteen years, Marcus Licinius Crassus was born the son of a senator and censor. His family, though perhaps not wealthy, ended up being well respected in Roman political groups.

As a youth Crassus was generally viewed as above reproach in nearly all categories save one: avarice. This weakness was seen most notably by Cicero. Pursuit of wealth is the best documented aspect of his life, along with other accomplishments shrinking in contrast. The vast fortune that Crassus possessed had been accrued mostly through the purchase of property in a variety of forms. The control of large amounts of slaves and mines also paid their own dividends. His primary concern in the Triumvirate was to gain favorable legislation for taxation in relation to his farming ventures in Asia. He also sought to keep an eye on the actions of his old rival Pompey, so that he could attempt to prevent him from gaining too much power in relation to his own. Beyond these two goals, Crassus's primary aim appears to be the accumulation of more wealth. His exploits to this end were frequently recorded in Plutarch's writing, the "Ufe of Crassus". It was this goal that would ultimately play a large part in leading to his death at the hands of the Parthians in 53 BC.

There are large portions of Crassus's early political life that are not known, though he did spend a period in exile around 80 BC. His brother and father were also killed during Marian proscriptions. During the civil war he served under Sulla in Africa, and proved himself quite capable on the field of battle. His later military career proved to be essentially limited to his victory over Spartacus, which was then stolen by Pompey. It would appear that Crassus preferred the economic and political arenas to that of warfare. He continued to work his way up through the ranks before being elected praetor in 73 BC and consul in 70 BC. For the next decade, Crassus and Pompey were engaged in a competition for supremacy in Rome, with Pompey ultimately standing victorious

Crassus was known for owning skilled slaves or employing talented tradesmen that would repair or reconstruct structures in poor condition. They would be transformed into expensive and lavish homes, which he would then sell for great profit. Crassus remained in Rome, continuing to exert his control though his finances. It was this powerful influence that repeatedly brought him into contact with Caesar. By the time Pompey returned back from the East in 61 BC, Caesar and Crassus had already become familiar to one another. Caesar was becoming an increasingly influential politician, while Crassus had the vast resources required to support Caesar's governmental career. The very first foundations of the Triumvirate were therefore laid into place well before the entrance of Pompey.

The Reign and Ruin of the Triumvirate

The specific time when the Triumvirate officially bound all three men together is unknown, though it is likely that it occurred before Caesar's election to the consulship rather than afterward.

Caesar was elected consul with the ineffective Bibulus as his counterpart. Pompey's desired agrarian law was passed, as were laws and regulations for the relief from overzealous tax farmers for Crassus. Caesar then dominated Roman politics for the year. It had been also during this span of twelve months that Caesar gave his child Julia to Pompey to wed, sealing his alliance in an exceedingly tangible means. All was likely proceeding according to plan. Yet only a decade later, the alliance would end in a catastrophic meltdown. The problem began in part with the death of Julia. The wedge was driven even further when Caesar traveled to Gaul at the conclusion of his consular term.

Pompey was fully aware of Caesar's actions during his campaign in Gaul. While Caesar was away, Pompey introduced legislation that rewarded the soldiers from his eastern campaigns with lands to farm. Caesar had many informers in the capital, as well as Senators that kept him apprised of what Pompey was up to. It is evident however that Pompey believed that Caesar could not see what he was doing and had no sources of military intelligence. His own lack of knowledge and colossal ego were coupled with an inferiority complex that turned their rivalry into a powder keg. This was not immediately evident, but over time it would present itself.

Caesar was aware of the risks related to leaving Rome for long periods of time, and sought to reduce this danger by becoming closer to Pompey. Crassus had appeared to have outlived his usefulness to Caesar, since the support of his allies had already been secured through his military conquests and taxation legislation. Pompey was nevertheless needed to a greater extent, not least of all because he still held considerable military and political power. In the year 59 BC he almost certainly still outmatched Caesar when it comes to resources. This instability was not to last, however.

Over the next years Caesar enjoyed great success in Gaul, accumulating wealth far beyond what his debts had been. A lot of this wealth he sent back to Rome, together with his famous memoirs written on his campaigns. The end result was that his prestige among the 'populares' and also the 'populus' in general continued to grow, while Pompey's own fame started to wane. Of the money that remained with Caesar, ample quantities were given to his soldiers for loyalty and effective service. By rewarding his troops, Caesar went even further to bolster his power. Their loyalty in essence made them into his military, not Rome's. It was to have great consequences leading up to the outbreak of civil war in 49 BC.

During the span of Caesar's absence from Roman politics, which lasted from about 58 to 56 BC, Pompey was struggling to maintain the position he felt he deserved as the First Man in Rome. At the beginning of 58 BC, Pompey again regressed from political life, pleased to spend time together with his brand new spouse. This was finally the opportunity required by his governmental opponents to start to undermine his authority. This occurred most notably with the tribune Clodius, who after spending a year attempting to repeal Pompey's legislation, directly opposed him at the trial of Milo in 56 BC. Whenever Pompey attempted to speak in the defense of Milo he was drowned away by Clodius and his men, who mocked him freely with insults of all kinds. Pompey was as a result highly distressed by these events. He was unused to receiving verbal punishment from anyone. What disturbed him even more was that neither the Senate nor Crassus had decided to support him. It's at the moment that Pompey began to become increasingly mistrustful. He was convinced that Crassus was plotting to have him killed, along with numerous other senators and magistrates.

    There likely was some part of truth to his suspicions, though it's doubtful that death was their aim for him: general public disgrace and loss of power would accomplish plenty. This series of incidents is immensely important whenever discussing the eventual rift that would form between Caesar and Pompey. Even his relations with Crassus had deteriorated to point where they were political opponents once again.

In 56 BC, Caesar called his meeting at Luca. Though he didn't really go back to Rome during his meeting, he was again briefly involved in Roman politics. Caesar never actually left Roman politics: he merely made his wishes known and enforced them through his various tribunes and other magistrates. Caesar's delegation of power allowed him to focus nearly entirely on his campaigns in Gaul.

Pompey started to entertain ideas of reconciling with all the optimates, with the expectation that he then would be in a prime position to regain his "rightful place" at the top of Rome. Caesar was aware of the deteriorating situation back in Rome and was worried, as with no support of Pompey and Crassus he would be at risk of losing his command. Therefore in the wintertime of 66 BC, Caesar met again with both Crassus and Pompey. The three renewed the pact of their Triumvirate. Additionally it was decided that Crassus and Pompey would be the consuls in 55 BC. His election would be secured by contingents of Caesar's men who were to be released to vote in the elections. Then when the consular term had ended, the two men were to be granted commands that would equal Caesar's. Caesar's own command was to be lengthened in order for all three men to have their terms expire at the same time. The final condition would be fulfilled in an attempt to relieve the growing power disparity between Caesar and the other two men. With disaster thus averted on this temporary basis, Caesar returned to his campaigns in Gaul.

 This conference was necessary for multiple reasons. First, Caesar bought himself time with which to prepare for the inevitable end of his command in Gaul. When it ended, he would inevitably be forced to defend himself against the various political opponents seeking to destroy him. Secondly, Caesar simultaneously established himself as the dominant position in the trio and calmed the rising tension between the other two.

If he lost his command, he would be vulnerable to charges brought against him for his heavy-handed and frequently unlawful actions during his consulship. While Appian and Plutarch declare that Pompey and Crassus both met Caesar at Luca, Cicero, in his letter to Spinther, seems to suggest that Crassus met with Caesar at Ravenna, and didn't join the later meeting at Luca. Whichever is correct, the outcome continues to be the same.

Pompey might not have normally permitted himself to be sent traveling at the behest of the man he regarded as lesser in status to him, but he was under immense pressure. As for Crassus, this now renewed contract actually elevated his position in the Triumvirate. It also gave him the opportunity to achieve what he had always desired: to eclipse Pompey though his own exploits. It stands to reason that Crassus left the conference completely satisfied.

With the agreement settled and the meeting convened, the Triumvirate was back on course. Crassus and Pompey headed back home to Rome. After the extended delay of their trip, they succeeded in the elections and then gained the consulship for the year 55 BC.

Everything was finally going exactly to plan for the three men, when the first in a series of blows rocked the Triumvirate. Pompey's beloved wife Julia died during childbirth, and the infant passed away soon after. That tragic event placed a significant stress upon Pompey and Caesar, both individually and in their relationship with one another. What should have been an event to strengthen their bond became one that nullified all physical connections between them. Even Caesar's later offer for Pompey to re-marry into his family did little to restore their connection, and it was subsequently rejected. While it is worth mentioning that while Julia's death was a great blow to the lasting stability of the Triumvirate, it by no means caused the final collapse. What it did do was yet again bring Pompey's worst weakness to the forefront: his own insecurity and the tenuous position of his status. With the loss of Crassus later in the same year, the Triumvirate would effectively be finished. Plutarch states that Caesar and Pompey had stayed together through mutual fear of what exactly Crassus might do if they turned upon one another. Crassus was no longer the active threat to either, and they knew it.

At this point there was little trust or faith between them. Pompey then decided to hedge his bets again, as Plutarch mentions, by gathering his power though metropolitan magistrates. What followed was a series of bargains and bribery as each man tried to secure the support of as many magistrates as possible. What Pompey didn't recognize was that Caesar had been developing and maintaining his power in the city for a long time. Even though Pompey had his own supporters, Caesar still had the definite advantage. The governmental environment in Rome by 54 BC had quickly approached that of chaos. The rule of law was practically nonexistent, and there were many who began to call for a dictator to be appointed to revive order. Pompey seemed like the most likely prospect to many in Rome, including Cato, who ultimately struggled with the notion of electing a dictator.

Plutarch mentions that Pompey's friends then came forward and defended the proconsul, stating that he had no desire to have the dictatorship thrust upon him. By denying that he had any aims at the dictatorship Pompey saw his credibility grow, and this soon silenced many of his critics. As the unease in Rome continued, the alliance between Caesar and Pompey began following an identical path. In 53 BC Caesar offered his great-niece Octavia to Pompey, hoping to once again solidify his pact through wedding, but Pompey declined. It appears odd that Pompey would have rejected such a clear overture of support unless he had been entertaining political advances through the optimates.

He instead married the daughter of the noblest man in Rome, Quintus Caecilius Metellus Pius Scipio Nasica. That marriage and the events of the year as a whole proved instrumental in the rift that grew even wider between Pompey and Caesar. The anarchy that had plagued Rome for nearly ten years reached a peak in that year, culminating with the murder of Clodius as well as the subsequent burning of the senate.

In the ensuing wave of violence and city-wide panic, the populus cried out for Pompey to be elected dictator or consul. A proposal was brought forth and Cato, the man who embodied the heart of the optimates, supported the nomination of Pompey as consul without a colleague. That the ever-so moral Cato might have supported such a blatantly unlawful work is amazing. It seems reasonable to assume that the optimates, seeing the current deterioration of their strength, decided to look to Pompey as an ally. It is commonly maintained that Pompey was still undecided on the topic of dictatorship at this time, but Cato's support of Pompey's power, combined with soon to follow wedding to a powerful optimus' daughter seems to indicate otherwise.

Up in Gaul, Caesar was understandably fully occupied with Vercingetorix's revolt. This marks perhaps the first time in his proconsulship that he left his supporters in Rome to largely do his fighting for him. Pompey, regardless of his individual feelings, was sticking to his promise of blocking conversation of Caesar's provinces until the year 50 BC, but that was only a portion of his plan. He additionally passed a new law whereby there would be a twelve month waiting duration for Consuls to take their provinces. As the legislation seemed legitimately made to curb electoral corruption, it left Caesar extremely vulnerable. He could now be replaced in his provinces as soon as 49 BC from the pool of available proconsuls, making him without imperium or public office for a complete twelve months before he could assume the consulship.

    Cato had long before sworn to prosecute Caesar instantly upon his loss of imperium, and it soon became apparent to everybody involved that this would be the undoing of Caesar, should it come to pass. Caesar himself was doing all he could to completely pacify Gaul before that time arrived, as he desired to have the ability to focus his undivided attention to politics when that time arrived. He knew that Pompey would not help him for much longer, and even though he hoped otherwise, he was preparing himself for the worst. From Pompey's third consulship onward, there can be few questions as to where his priorities lay. Though he did secure Caesar the right to the office of consul in absentia, he essentially nullified that when combined with his anti-corruption legislation. Moreover, he passed a resolution whereby Caesar and he would each send one legion to secure the protection of the borders in the East. While seemingly reasonable, both legions were in fact from Caesar's very own army, as Pompey had years prior lent one of his own Spanish legions to Caesar. This final act in particular stands as an obvious instance of reducing Caesar's power in order to limit his options. It would appear that civil war was a continuing worry of the senate, and though Pompey discovered the idea preposterous, he had been always ready to increase his own power over his rival.

    The true irony of Pompey's political place is the fact that he never might have experienced control of so much power, had not the risk of Caesar been perceived as so high in Rome. In Pompey the optimate senators saw someone that would guard them against Caesar's aspirations, as long as they fed his ego and strengthened his insecurities. While Pompey thought he had finally become part of the inner elite that he had strove his entire life to become, he had been merely an instrument. Pompey was supported by the optimates because they believed he was not a threat to Rome and would be easily controlled. This stood in stark contrast to the dangerous enigma that was Caesar. By 50 BC the Triumvirate had truly crumbled, in both name and actuality. All that was left was for the optimates and Pompey to goad Caesar into crossing the Rubicon, sparking the second civil war in half a century. Caesar tread in the footsteps of many before him and used the military to achieve his own ambitions in the Roman capitol. This was a major turning point in Roman history.

Could these two very different men - with their own desire for power and substantial egos - have gotten along indefinitely had events occurred differently? Certainly not. Both lusted for similar positions, with exactly the same recognition, but both could not achieve it. There could be only one First Man in Rome.

Pompey, though he thought he had achieved this great honor, was in fact a mere puppet to the optimates. They had showered him with platitudes to receive his support. The populus, to whom Pompey was still a well-regarded hero, did much to strengthen his impression that he was needed by Rome. The roles of power had been reversed. The adulation that Caesar received from his troops was no false impression: he had been a leader that inspired real respect. He knew this, and demanded to be addressed accordingly. When he was not, this left him with only one decision to make; he would not bow to the opposition. There was only one possible outcome, and that was his own sole and complete victory. The partnership had started with three, been reduced to two, and then finally only one remained. Now there was only Caesar.

Chapter 5: Civil War in Rome

The balance of power within the Roman Republic had been upset. At this point, Crassus was fighting in Syria against the Parthians, a somewhat nomadic people who lived primarily in the Iranian and Mesopotamian areas. Their soldiers were master archers on horseback, firing upon their enemies while remaining out of range. In 53 BC Crassus and his men fell into a trap at Carrhae and most were slaughtered. Caesar and Pompey were now the only two left. Their relationship had been strained already by the death of Caesar's daughter Julia who was also Pompey's wife only a year before. Pompey was not in Spain, instead commanding from Rome where he gradually shifted his aspirations towards the senatorial party. Pompey liked to show himself to be traditional and honest, and a follower of the laws. Whether his character had changed or if this was only an act we do not know, however he and Caesar had already taken numerous illegal actions. There was now a precedent that reinforced disrespect of the law. Caesar and Pompey openly took up illegal consulships and even ignored the vetoes of their colleagues. Even during the most successful period of the Triumvirate's power, street gangs backed by powerful politicians were known for getting out of control.

One such infamous example was Publius Clodius, who was at one point in pursuit of a personal vendetta against Cicero, forcing him into exile with threats and bullying for a time. He was crafty and used many stratagems to achieve his goals. He also sought to become tribune and distributed grain to the citizens of Rome in an effort to gain their support. His misdeeds came to an abrupt end in January 52 BC when he was murdered by the street thugs of another faction. In the ensuing fighting in the streets, the Senate house was burned to the ground and chaos reigned. So great was the confusion that no consuls were elected. Pompey was not trusted enough for the Senate to appoint him dictator, but he served as the sole consul and managed to restore order. Pompey used his influence to legally but disloyally renew his own command, but made no attempt to prevent Caesar from being recalled when his five years were up. Cicero saw the crisis was imminent as Caesar began his return. He accurately summed up the situation: "Pompey is determined that Caesar shall not become consul unless he hands over his army and provinces; Caesar is convinced that he will never be safe if he relinquishes his army."

The Senate passed an emergency decree of 'Senatus consultum ultimum', the same decree they had used previous to execute Gaius Gracchus, Catiline, and others without trials. Caesar had to make a decision. Caesar brought his army with him instead of entering Italy powerless, breaking the law in the process of crossing the Rubicon. Civil wars claimed the next nineteen years, lasting until 30 BC, and ending with the destruction of the Republic. Pompey was surprised by Caesar's advance into Italy. Only two legions remained in the Peninsula, but he and his allies had many forces standing by in Spain. Other parts of the empire were controlled by the senatorial party. Pompey barely managed to escape to the east and beat the rapid advance of Caesar. Pompey's past triumph had helped him create a vast network of supporters and allies. Caesar had quickly overrun Italy, and defeated the Pompeians in Spain before crossing the Adriatic and challenging Pompey. Caesar attempted to blockade Dyrrhachium, but his efforts failed and the situation grew grim. The tide changed for Caesar when Pompey unwisely made the decision to give battle at Pharsalus in Greece in 48 BC. Pompey's forces outnumbered him, but Caesar's veterans had been tested in the fires of war for ten long years in Gaul, and they completely annihilated Pompey's army.

Pompey had no choice but to flee to Egypt, but he was promptly murdered upon arrival by those seeking to gain favor with the winning side. Caesar reportedly regretted the death of his former friend, and executed his assassins. Interestingly, Pompey enjoyed acclaim and a generally honored role in Roman culture for the next several hundred years.

Caesar arrived in Alexandria and quickly became involved in an Egyptian dispute. He proved instrumental in placing the 21-year-old Cleopatra upon the throne. Cleopatra later became his mistress and bore a son named Caesarion, whom she maintained was his. Caesar headed back to Italy and routed Pharnaces of Pontus (the son of Mithridates) at the battle of Zela. This was the famous battle where Caesar coined the phrase, "I came, I saw, I conquered".

He next traveled from Italy into Africa and defeated the remaining forces of Pompey at Thapsus. Cato was among the forces and he chose to commit suicide rather than be captured by Caesar. Caesar was nearly defeated in 45 BC at the last stand of Pompey's forces at Munda in Spain. Only the raw tenacity of his legionaries led him to victory over the sons of Pompey. In four short years Caesar had completely conquered the Roman world and changed it forever. He occasionally returned to Rome and enacted new reforms, including founding a new colony for his veterans from the Gaul campaigns, as well as setting up a new tax system. Additionally, he introduced the 365 day Julian calendar.

    He had accumulated as much authority as legitimately the Roman system could bestow. Though Republican government forms were not meddled with, Julius Caesar proceeded to go much further than Sulla: he was voted dictator for life, his portrait was seen on Roman coins, he wore a imperial garment and other quasi royal emblems, the month of July was named after him, and the possibility developed that he aspired to divinity, which had been something prevalent among Greek rulers from Alexander the Great on forward. He even permitted a temple to be devoted toward him.

Contemporaries appear to have supposed that in him Rome had at long last discovered an important and long ruling master, different from men like Marius, Pompey, or even Sulla, whose long-term aims had not gone beyond a preponderant influence in the state based on prestige, wealth and a network of Roman and provincial clients. Caesar on his own never changed the conventional framework of the Republic and in 44 BC refused the title King, detested by Romans ever since the sovereignty of Tarquinius Superbus; but his style of government was more and more autocratic, and prompted the conspiracy that contributed to his murder, at the age of 56, on the Ides of March, 44 BC.

One of Caesar's most appealing qualities was his magnanimity: he in many instances spared conquered opponents during the course of the Civil War, and often took them into his service. This very much praised clemency appears to have applied only to Romans: large quantities of defeated Gauls lost their right hands for standing up to Caesar, and in addition Vercingetorix was strangled and flung all the way down from the Tarpeian Rock below the capitol. Caesar appears to have been ultimately undone by his virtue rather than his ambition: the principal assassins, Brutus and Cassius, were ex-Pompeians that Caesar had earlier spared. Crowding together around him as if they were petitioners, they stabbed him to death as he was just about to attend a conference of the legislature. Around the time he was preparing to venture on a new campaign in the East, versus the Parthians; although his demise has now and again been said to have prevented Caesar from bringing about a golden age of great government, this actuality indicates that he was above all a compulsive conqueror. Caesar's demise settled nothing, for the Republic was too far gone to be saved. Regardless of the odd version of history made familiar by Shakespeare in Julius Caesar, the Caesarean political party carried out no immediate attack to avenge their chief's death;

the dictator's most important lieutenant, Mark Antony, consented to pardon the assassins, and it was the outrage of the citizens that drove Brutus and Cassius from Rome. Affairs were further complicated by the appearance of Caesar's nephew and eventual successor, the 18-year-old Octavian, who ended up being at one point at war with fellow Caesarean Mark Antony. However, they came to the realization that by pooling their military resources they could over-awe the Senate, a plan of action all the more enticing while Brutus and Cassius had started to gain control of the East. In 43 BC, Antony and Octavian established the Second Triumvirate, bringing in Lepidus, a follower of Caesar who controlled parts of Gaul as well as Spain. Unlike the First Triumvirate, this new fusion had obtained an official position as a five-year, three man dictatorship, legitimately sanctioned by the now subservient Senate. The Triumvirate did certainly not think twice to slay their enemies, including the 63-year-old Cicero, who had prematurely cheered Caesar's killing and denounced Antony. In 42 BC, Brutus and Cassius were beaten near Philipi, after which each committed suicide.

In the subsequent separation of the Roman world, Octavian acquired the West; by 36 BC he had managed to defeat Pompey's son, Sextus Pompeius - who had been holding out inside Sicily - and to seize control of Africa from Lepidus. Lepidus was actually a lucky failure in a blood soaked age: he had been permitted to withdraw into private life. Together with the elimination of the other contenders, Octavian and Antony were probably fated to battle for supremacy in the Roman domain. The conflict was more than once postponed by gatherings and new arrangements, in spite of Antony's increasingly un-Roman behavior. Though he previously married his rival's sister Octavia, he became more and more closely involved with Cleopatra, queen of Egypt and Caesar's former mistress. She bore him three children, and their affair has frequently been depicted as a love story. Regardless of whether this had been so, their famous union had solid political advantages; it was put on a long-term basis in 36 BC, after Antony had undertaken a disastrous campaign against the Parthians, perhaps because he now viewed that Egypt's abundant resources were crucial to his political survival. Moreover Cleopatra was the last of the free Greek rulers, and as such commanded a good deal of loyalty in the Hellenized East as well as Egypt – loyalty that the partners tried to exploit by identifying themselves as Greek and Egyptian deities.

On the other hand, Antony's unconventional conduct – pointed up by territorial concessions to Egypt and the award of provinces to his Romano-Egyptian children – was bound to alienate his supporters in Italy and the Army, and may therefore have cost him his life. Since Caesar had been deified, his adopted son Octavian could style himself son of the God, but without forfeiting his credentials as a defender of Roman values. His propaganda made much of the oriental decadence to which Antony had been enticed, and when he declared war in 31 BC it was shrewdly upon the foreign temptress Cleopatra. The opponents met in northern Greece, where Octavian's general, Agrippa, outmaneuvered and hemmed in the enemy forces; Antony's desperate attempt to break out by sea at Actium was met with disaster. He and Cleopatra fled to Egypt where, deserted by his allies and followers, he killed himself as Octavian approached Alexandria. Rather than decorate Octavian's triumph, Cleopatra committed suicide. According to legend she allowed a poisonous asp snake to bite her.

In the immediate postwar settlement, Egypt was annexed; significantly, it became the personal property of the all-powerful Octavian, not a province belonging to Rome. Some of the legions were disbanded, and the Empire was at last peaceful and united again. Despite the bloodshed, the most important victim of the wars was the sovereignty of the Roman senate and people; and though Romans politely continued to pretend otherwise, the Republic was now dead.

Chapter 6: Death of the Republic

Octavian was probably the most levelheaded and clear-sighted leader in Roman history. He had climbed to greatness over the bodies of his opponents, like Sulla and Caesar before him; but once he held power he used it moderately, presenting himself as a guardian of tradition and capitalizing on the universal longing for peace and order after generations of turmoil. He also had a gift often lacking in great leaders: the gift for discovering able and willing servants. Since he could not be everywhere, Octavian employed Gaius Maecenas as his political man-of-all work and diplomatic troubleshooter; and, being a general himself, he found a first class general in Marcus Agrippa, who was mainly responsible for the great naval victories over Sextus Pompeius and Mark Antony.

Having restored order and reformed the state, Octavian formally handed back control to the Senate and people in 27 BC: the Senate would function as before, elected consuls would carry out its wishes, and the people would be represented by their tribunes. Octavian did not assume the dictatorship, contenting himself with a recognized preeminence; as well as bearing the honorary title of princeps, the chief, he was now to be officially distinguished from other citizens as Augustus - the name by which has become best known - and given special responsibilities and powers to assist in the ordering of the state. In reality this restoration of the Republic was a sham, though perhaps a beneficent one that was used in an inevitable transition. Augustus possessed the overwhelming military force, wealth and prestige that made his word law; and like his uncle he was becoming the object of religious cults. Accumulating offices he was able with perfect legality to remove recalcitrant senators, to appoint new members, and to prevent troublemakers from ever reaching the

Senate. He was granted a permanent tribunal power including an absolute veto, so that even the weapons of the popular party were forced to serve the new absolutism; and as supreme commander of the armed forces he controlled the provinces in which they were stationed, ruling through legates directly appointed by him instead of governors nominated by the Senate. Eventually he even became the religious head of state.

In the wake of the civil wars, Romans seem to have been content with these arrangements. Augustus's reign was one of harmony between rulers and ruled, in which the question of an appeal to ultimate authority or force scarcely rose; but he is rightly described not as the restorer of the Republic but as the first of the Roman emperors. The permanence of the new system was ensured by Augustus's ability, and the tact with which he handled the Senate and respected traditional forms. By this accident of longevity, he gave the Roman world a single master for over 40 years. By the time of his death, the old institutions had long before lost the habit of asserting themselves. Under Augustus, the Empire enjoyed peace, order and prosperity. A proper civil service was created to run it, giving good government to the provinces as well as to Rome. New roads and colonies encouraged industry and commerce. Devolution of authority - albeit mainly in routine matters - breathed fresh life into the cities. Augustus gradually eliminated the Army as a political force by greatly reducing its numbers and distributing it all through the frontier provinces; in Italy, the few thousand men of the Praetorian Guard, an elite corps created by Augustus for his personal protection, constituted the sole military presence. Rome itself was transformed into a worthy capitol for a universal empire: Augustus wrote that he had found it a city of brick and left it a city of marble. He also left it efficiently supplied with water and food, minimizing the risk of political discontent: 200,000 people received a free corn dole and were entertained by ever more extravagant public spectacles – the celebrated policy of keeping the people happy with bread and circuses. The Empire continued to expand. Julius Caesar had conquered Western Europe as far as the Rhine; under Augustus the conquest of an area roughly corresponding to modern Austria and Hungary brought the Roman frontier and Eastern Europe to the Danube. The Rhine and the Danube were to remain the frontiers in Europe for another hundred years; Augustus's intention to push on to the Elbe was abandoned near the end of his reign, when three legions under the legate Varus – perhaps 15,000 men – were ambushed and wiped out in the Teutoburg Forest. This was the greatest catastrophe of his reign, and it was said that Augustus left his hair and beard untrimmed for months afterward and often beat his head against the door, crying out 'Quinctilius Varus, give me back my legions!' As if infected with permanent bad luck, the three legions were never reconstituted. Augustus's advice to his successors was to attempt no further expansion.

However, despite the setback the frontiers were later stabilized in Africa and the East as well as Europe, and honor was satisfied when it comes to war when the Parthians agreed to return the Roman Standards they had captured in defeating Crassus at Carrhae.

Augustus was fortunate even in the literary history of his reign, which produced the poets Virgil and Horace and the historian Livy. All three were encouraged and generously funded by Maecenas, whose name is still often used in English to characterize the wealthy and enlightened patron. However genuine his appreciation of talent, Maecenas also used patronage as a way of securing politically acceptable views of the state of the Empire and the role of Augustus. Virgil, in the Aeneid, the greatest of Roman epics, inserted laudatory references to Caesar Augustus, son of a god, and to Rome's splendid imperial destiny, into his account of the Romans mythical ancestor. By contrast, the other great poet of the Augustan age was a younger man, Ovid, the author of elegantly worldly verses; whether for this reason or as punishment for some other offense, he ended his life in exile.

Ovid's playfully amoral outlook was certainly not to Augustus's taste. The emperors traditionalism was genuine enough in most respects although not where the tradition of liberty was concerned. He circulated ostentatiously pious images of himself, restored religious rites that have been neglected in favor of Greek and Oriental practices, and tried to revive the old Roman virtues by decree. The luxuries of the upper classes were rebuked and legislated against; marriage and paternity were encouraged; and Augustus even exiled his own daughter Julia when he found out about her lurid sex life. Like most such endeavors, this policy showed few positive results.

But the most serious of Augustus's family troubles was the succession. He and his wife Livia had no children, although Livia's son by an earlier marriage, Tiberius, became one of the mainstays of the Roman state, both as an administrator and an able and tireless campaigner. The younger men whom Augustus groomed to succeed him died in such abnormal numbers that even in antiquity there were rumors pointing to Livia as an arch-murderess on Tiberius's behalf; whether they were more than malicious gossip is another matter, despite the ingenuity's of Robert Graves's famous novel "I, Claudius". In any event Augustus was finally compelled to name Tiberius as his successor; when he died in 14 AD, there was no serious possibility of a restoration of the Republic, although the 56-year-old Tiberius for a time resisted, with real or assumed vigor, the Senate's invitation to carry on the principate. Augustus's final apotheosis was a literal one – to be recognized and worshiped as a god, giving his political system the ultimate sanction of religious endorsement.

The reign of Tiberius from 14 - 37 AD was in most respects a conservative continuation of the Augustine. The administration of the provinces was, if anything, improved; there was little military activity; and the frontiers remained the same apart from the continuation of a process begun under Augustus, the absorption of the client kingdoms of Asia minor and the East. Though able, Tiberius seems to have been an unsympathetic personality, and in the early years of his reign he was far less popular than his nephew Germanicus, who appears to have cultivated a personal following in Rome. When Germanicus died while on a special mission at Antioch, rumors circulated that Tiberius had had him poisoned; the rumors may have been unfounded, but suggest that the atmosphere of intrigue and suspicion, characteristic of autocracies, had begun to thicken.

In time the dangers inherent in autocracy became still clearer. After 23 AD the Emperor delegated wide powers to Sejanus, the prefect of the Praetorian Guard, who carried out many judicial murders in pursuit of his own ambitions and may have done away with Tiberius's own son Drusus. In 26 AD Tiberius retired permanently to the island of Capri, where he is said to have indulged in infamous orgies; but since the stories, like many accounts of the emperors, come from gossip loving or nostalgically Republican writers, they may be exaggerated or even false: Tiberius's residence on Capri, and his feeble or indifferent reaction to the string of treason trials that disfigured his reign, are just as likely to have been the result of old age, since he was 68 in the year 26 AD. It could have been Sejanus's plotting that was responsible for the executions of Agrippina (the wife of Germanicus) and two of her children, even though they were Tiberius's heirs. But the aged Emperor could still act decisively when he felt threatened, as he showed by summarily executing Sejanus and instituting a long series of treason trials that eliminated the following popular rivals and possibly many innocent victims. Tiberius's death in 37 AD was greeted with the joy and relief that proved to be premature.

Chapter 7: Reigns of Terror

There are fewer doubts about the character of Tiberius's successor Gaius, nicknamed Caligula (meaning little boot) by the soldiers of his father Germanicus: he was insane, arbitrary and cruel, and the Republican institutions of Rome proved helpless to restrain him. Parading about and the deluded belief that he was already a God, he forced senators to commit suicide, tortured and put to death equestrians, soldiers and actors with crazy impartiality, executed any wealthy man who did not make him his heir, and ensured that his fall would be greeted with universal pleasure by raising heavy taxes on every imaginable commodity to make good the effects of his reckless spending. Among Caligula's caprices was the appointment of his horse as a senator and the building of the huge bridge of boats moored end to end across the Bay of Baiae. He did this because a would-be prophet once had once predicted that he was no more likely to become Emperor than he was to ride completely dry across the bay. It is said that every boat in Italy had been requisitioned to construct the bridge. This caused economic chaos while Caligula rode his horse back and forth across the bay, over the planks that had been laid between the ships.

Legally there was no way of resisting Caligula. The principate was revealed for the despotism it was, with the inescapable weakness of all despotisms – that there was no way of guaranteeing the benevolence, intelligence or even sanity of the despot. Caligula was murdered by conspirators in 41 AD, after a four-year reign of terror. His successor Claudius was ominously the choice of the praetorians. Although as Caligula's uncle he was also next in line for the succession, since the principate was now effectively a hereditary monarchy.

His undiagnosed disabilities made a public career impossible under Augustus and

Tiberius, since people in antiquity ridiculed physical disadvantages and equated them with stupidity or worse. On the other hand Claudius's disabilities may well have saved his life when Tiberius and Caligula were jealously cutting down relatives that might prove to be rivals. It has also been suggested that Claudius was shrewd enough to exaggerate his lack of physical ability in order to be passed over as harmless.

In any event, Claudius's reign from 41 AD to 54 AD was fairly successful, and there seems no reason to deprive him of the credit for its achievements. Though no soldier himself, he was generous and rewarded good service, including the service of Aulus Plautius, the Conqueror of Britain. The invasion of this remote island took place in 43 AD, and Claudius arrived in time to take part in the storming of the British capital, Colchester. Eventually the lowland zone of Britain – roughly modern England – was conquered and Romanized, while the highland areas of Scotland and part of Wales remained Celtic strongholds.

In the Empire, Claudius encouraged the extension of Roman citizenship, mainly through the foundation of colonies in the admission of Gallic nobles to the Roman Senate. The civil service was improved by Claudius's practice of employing freed men, although other Romans deplored their excessive influence. Several ancient authors believed that Claudius's freed men and his wife were actually the power behind the throne. The charge has a certain credibility. Even after the spectacular sexual antics of his young wife Messalina were revealed and paid for with her life, Claudius, almost 60, married again. His new Empress, Agrippina, then persuaded him to adopt her son Nero as his heir; and four years later Claudius died – conveniently, since Nero, not yet 17, was old enough to inherit the throne unlike his stepbrother Claudius and Messalina's son Britannicus but still young enough to let himself be ruled by his mother.

Rumor had it that the uxorious Claudius expired after partaking from a wifely dish of poisoned mushrooms. After his demise Claudius was deified; Nero, in a flash of black humor, is said to have called mushrooms the food of the gods.

Nero, if not quite mad, proved to be recklessly cruel and blindly vain. At first under the influence of his mother, who's head even appeared with Nero on his coins, he soon put himself under the tutelage of the philosopher Seneca and the praetorian prefect Burrus, who ruled competently in his name. But after this deceptively quiet start Nero increasingly took over the reins. He did away with Britannicus and his overweening mother; treason trials were revived to raise money from the victim's estates; and when this led to the formation of a genuine conspiracy, it's discovery set Nero off on a paranoid round of executions in which any popular soldier or administrator was likely to be killed or order to take his own life. The disastrous fire which destroyed part of Rome in

64 AD has been blamed on Nero, possibly unjustly, although the Emperor chose to accuse the small, obscure sect of Christians and, instead of replacing the destroyed tenements and temples, erected a vast palace complex, the Golden house, on the site.

The charge that Nero fiddled while Rome burned (actually that he sang The Fall of Troy), accompanying himself on the lyre may only be gossip but is absolutely in character: he had a mania for art, and went in for extremes of temperament and self dramatization.

In 64 AD the residence of Rome primarily lived in wooden houses and shacks, which were easy prey for fire when so densely populated in urban centers. Fire broke out under the full moon one night in July and the Roman historian Tacitus recorded it, though he was only a small child at that point. The chariot racing stadium known as the Circus Maximus was the first building to burn. The wind picked up, fanning the flames and quickly turning it into an inferno.

The fire spread through the narrow streets and in the tight alleyways. The city erupted in chaos and he heard terrified screams of people. Large crowds of confused citizens stumbled out into the streets, blocking the paths of escape and leaving children and elderly helpless. Many attempted to just get away, and some tried bravely to fight the fires or to save others. The Roman appointed firefighters had their efforts hindered by gangs who wanted to watch the city burn. There were even some who screwed torches, and set fires themselves. It is unclear whether or not they were ordered to this or purely wanted to see the city burn. The fire raged for five days when the demolition of all the buildings and a large area around the Esquiline Hill seem to have stopped the fire, but it furiously broke out again and spread even more widely. By the time the fire finally died, a significant portion of the city was severely damaged and much of it completely destroyed. Modern records record that as much as one tenth to two thirds of the city was devastated by the fire. Records do not indicate how many people lost their businesses because of the fires, but it is likely significant because of how densely populated businesses and tenements were.

Nero was away at the Antium coast when the fire first broke out. To his credit, he returned to Rome and some relief effort was organized. What is unclear is whether or not this was the effort of his advisers or Nero himself. History and his contemporaries had a more negative view and typically do not give him this credit. Those citizens who had lost their homes were granted permission to camp in public spaces as well as public works, such as gardens. The price of corn was lowered and many supplies of food were brought in from other neighboring towns.

However, the rumor began to spread the Emperor was seen in the home of friends singing about the fires and destruction of Troy. People began to believe that this fire had been deliberately started by Nero so he could glorify himself by rebuilding it in his own name as a new city he imagined. Many authors have given accounts that the fire was deliberately started, while some believed that it was only a terrible accident. When Nero heard that people believed that he had started the fires, he quickly took action. The Christian population was blamed and were quickly rounded up. They were tortured to the point of forced (and likely false) confession, and subsequently fed while still alive to dogs, who proceeded to tear them to pieces. Many other Christians were crucified and some were burned alive and used as torches along the roadways at night.

    He further shocked the Romans by making public appearances on the stage, and preferred spending his time in Greece, where he carried off a string of prizes as a lyricist and charioteer. The judges were presumably biased – as biased as the historian Suetonius opposite direction when he claims that during Nero's performances no one was permitted to leave the theater, and consequently women gave birth there and men who were dying of boredom pretended to die in earnest so that they would be carried outside.

Nero's reign of terror had to end. Gaul, Spain and Africa soon rose against the Romans. Nero's antics continued, and he could think of no remedy except singing while his Empire burned. The Praetorian Guards deserted him. After attempts to flee proved ineffective, he took his own life at the age of 30 in 68 AD.

In life, Nero was known for his terrible spells of rage. He was erratic and at one point killed his own mother, his wife, and many others. He began performing in public and the people and senators reacted poorly to it. On one particular occasion, his second wife mentioned a mistake he had made during the performance. The comment made him so violently angry that he kicked her to death in a fit of rage. After the fire Rome was severely damaged. Many senators even suggested that the capitol should be moved to a different city. Nero decided to rebuild the capitol city of Rome. It was this decision that in large part contributed to his downfall. This rebuilding project was so massive that he used large sums from the treasury. Soon the treasury's resources ran out and he came up with new ways of getting money. Nero was seen by many as a bully and he began to take money from the temples as well as raising taxes. In some occasions he even found ways of legally stealing money from the rich. He soon became even more unpopular, this time losing support among even the Senators and ruling elite.

    Nero had a childlike love of entertainment that was contrasted by his acts of incredible cruelty. As he grew increasingly poorer, his citizens also grew increasingly poor. Many resorted to violence to support themselves. He was deeply unpopular. One of the greatest criticisms of Nero was the golden house that he had built. It was seen as frivolous and greedy spending, but the construction was even more scandalous because it was built on the land cleared out after the great fire of Rome. Instead of rebuilding the city itself, he destroyed the remnants of the homes in the wake of the fire and directed a structure dedicated to himself. Ultimately his advisors and people rebelled against him. His arrogance and narcissism combined with his apparent mental instability proved to be his downfall. Nero is a shocking example that not all leaders should be in positions of power, nor are they suited for the task. After his death, a once great dynasty came to and inglorious end.

The rule of Nero was followed by Servius Sulpicius Galba, the former Governor of Spain. He was considered the most obvious candidate for the job. He, like many others in the past, marched on Rome and when he arrived he changed his title from governor to that of Caesar. There were many others within the city who were vying for the role of Caesar. Because of this knowledge that he had multiple contenders also vying for this position, he felt threatened. He instigated a new series of purges, murdering his rivals indiscriminately, and this did little to endear him in the minds of the Roman public. In fact, he was hated for the exact same reasons as Nero.

Time proved that he would make many of the same mistakes. He angered many powerful players in Roman politics, including senior officials in the Army and the Praetorian Guard. He had initially secured his position and authority by promising bonuses and additional benefits for those serving in the Armed Forces, but once he took his throne he went back on those promises.

Most in the Army were furious, and many in the legions demanded fair reward, especially after just having crushed an uprising in France. Eventually, the Praetorian Guard rose against him when his purges begin to dip into the Praetorian Guard ranks. The Roman people were plagued by bad ruler after bad ruler. Each was focused more on their own power and well-being than the needs of their people. The history of Rome however is punctuated by men who were born for the task given to them. This eventually culminated in the five good emperors. These men managed to maintain peace and good government in Rome by refusing to continue with the established process for accession. Rather than passing the role down in a hereditary line, they instead gave power to the person they felt best deserved it. This most often was someone who had no ambition to rule and would use their power responsibly, and exercise restraint. With the exception of Marcus Aurelius, all of these leaders found individuals who they groomed to take power.

Chapter 8: The Collapse

The scandalous doings of the Caesars, which has almost certainly been exaggerated, had little effect on life in the provinces. The political classes at Rome were sometimes strained, but over most of the period between Augustus and Nero, the Empire was prosperous, well governed and at peace. The Pax Romana (Roman Peace) became the most widely recognized benefit conferred by the Empire. It could also be seen as justification for the Roman subjugation of other peoples. Violent outbreaks - such as the savage revolution of the Iceni under Boudicca - were unlikely, except in recently conquered or unstable provinces.

But the events following the death of Nero were to affect wide areas of the Empire, temporarily destroying its peace. Nero was the last of the Julio-Claudians, the dynasty formed by the Julian family, represented by Caesar and

Augustus, and the Claudians, relatives of Augustus's stepson Tiberius. There was now no obvious heir, and the throne was at the disposal of the Praetorian Guard – or of the legions in the provinces, who entered politics for the first time. 69 AD was the year of the four emperors, and reintroduced the empire to the miseries of civil war. The aged Galba, Governor of one of the Spanish provinces, rose to the throne. He was then murdered and replaced by his colleague Otho. Galba was conspired against by the Praetorian Guard. He was hacked to death in the forum by a group of soldiers. His adoptive son was also murdered. Galba's head was severed from his body, put on a stake, and paraded around the city for others to mock. But when the Rhine Army marched on behalf of Vitellius, Otho found himself deserted and committed suicide. Finally the Eastern Legions supported Vespasian, a tough and highly successful commander who was engaged at the time in suppressing a major Jewish rebellion. His forces overcame those of Vitellius, who was killed.

The serial blood-lettings demonstrated the danger of allowing the Army back into politics. They also confirmed that the Republic was beyond revival, even when the candidates for the Imperial throne appeared to be completely different from Julius Caesar or Octavian. Furthermore local and tribal outbreaks in Gaul and on the Rhine indicated that the stability of the Empire itself might be at risk as soon as the central power faltered. Fortunately Vespasian proved to be the strong leader the state required. Being of relatively humble birth he adopted the image of a plain, blunt man. He undertook a conciliatory line with the Senate, but he left them in no doubt that the Flavian family were to be the new ruling dynasty. He implicitly dismissed the Senate's endorsement by beginning his reign from when he was proclaimed Caesar by the Legions.

Mindful of the way in which he had attained power, Vespasian carefully controlled the Army, and his son Titus became Captain of the Praetorian Guard. Civic privileges and membership of the Senate were extended. Taxes had previously been pardoned by weaker Emperors to win themselves a short-lived popularity. Vespasian quickly put a stop to this and the debts were collected. In 70 AD Titus ended the Jewish revolt by destroying Jerusalem and the Temple. These events were so calamitous that for centuries pious Jews refused to pass under the arch of Titus, built to celebrate his victory. Vespasian died in 79 AD and was immediately deified. He evidently foresaw his elevation, making a final deathbed joke: "Damn it - I can feel myself turning into a God."

    The brief reign of Titus was notable for the completion of the vast arena known as the Colosseum. It was used for gladiatorial shows as well as animal hunts. The eruption of Vesuvius in 79 AD also occurred during his reign, and it smothered the seaside resorts of Pompeii and Herculaneum in the bay of Naples. Layers of ash and pumice choked the citizens and buried the towns, preserving a fascinating record of the Roman way of life. Titus was succeeded by his brother Domitian, who campaigned effectively and governed well for a few years. Political opposition led him to fear for his own safety, and this set in motion another epidemic of treason trials. Finally, when no one could feel safe, even Domitian's wife turned against him and joined a group of conspirators whose agents stabbed the Emperor to death. By this point it grew increasingly clear that holding a position of power exposed leaders to the machinations and plots of those who would take it from them.

The childless Domitian was the last of the Flavians, but this time the transition from one dynasty to the next was managed without an interval of bloodshed. The Senate nominated Nerva, an elderly member of their own order who had managed to remain respectable while conforming under emperors of widely different characters from Nero onward. Nerva kept the confidence of the Senate by promising to deal fairly with it and never to execute one of its members – a promise he kept even when a senator was implicated in a conspiracy against him. Nerva was also shrewd enough to adopt an experienced general, Trajan, as his son and successor. The Emperor's motive was probably to hold in check the Army, particularly the Praetorian Guard. They had admired Domitian and resented his removal. But the adoption brought such obviously beneficial results that it became something of a custom, and was followed by Trajan and his successors. At any rate it seems unlikely to have been an accident that each childless ruler selected a childless successor. The result was the succession of the Five Good Emperors. They were linked by ruling ability and character, not by blood. This gave the Empire one of the most efficient and humane governments it had ever had. The period is often described as the age of the Antonines, although strictly speaking the term should only apply to the fourth Emperor, Antonius Pius, and his successors.

Chapter 9: Five Good Emperors

Nerva's reign was brief, but Trajan had a long and energetic Imperial career from 98 to 117 A.D. Despite his Spanish birth, Trajan was a ruler very much to the Roman taste, taking command personally on the frontiers. When the Dacians beyond the Danube frontier, already punished by Domitian, sought their revenge, Trajan undertook a series of campaigns in 101-106 A.D. that culminated in the death of the Dacian king, the addition to the empire of a large, mineral rich province roughly corresponding to modern Romania, and loot on a scale that had not been seen for decades. Back in Rome, Trajan behaved as a model Emperor, maintaining good relations with the Senate, paying close attention to administrative business, and arranging for cheap loans to farmers, the payment of subsidies to the Italian poor, and other welfare measures. He also embarked on an ambitious building program, giving Rome one of her finest squares, the Forum Traianum, and Trajan's Market, an innovative complex best described as a multilevel shopping mall; in the Forum Traianum stood the most impressive of the Emperor's surviving monuments, Trajan's Column, with a vivid bronze sculpture picturing his campaigns against the Dacians. Understandably enthusiastic, the Senate awarded Trajan the official title 'Optimus Princeps' –'Best of Leaders'.

In the last years of his reign, Trajan won substantial victories in the East against the Parthians. He created two new provinces from his conquests: Armenia, and Mesopotamia in the relatively small northern part of the region. He then pressed on as far as the Persian Gulf. However, his ambitions outran his strength and he died in the East. His successor Hadrian (117 to 138 AD) took a very different view of the general situation, and his policies made it abundantly obvious that he believed the Empire was dangerously overextended. At the end of Trajan's life there were widespread revolts in his eastern conquests, and Hadrian quickly relinquished them. He spent most of his reign touring the empire, supervising provincial administrators, and overhauling the Legions. He tirelessly strengthened fortifications and recruited on the frontiers. One familiar result of this activity was Hadrian's Wall in northern Britain, a defensive structure that ran for 73 miles across the narrow neck of land between the Solway and the Tyne. Forts and signaling turrets positioned all along the wall were intended to prevent a successful surprise attack by the unconquered Celts of the far north. The Legions were no longer primarily responsible for the defense of the frontier borders. Auxiliaries were often recruited locally and used for this purpose instead.

Although his policies were essentially defensive, Hadrian was popular with the Army and provincials because he was energetic and seemed to be omnipresent. The most serious internal disturbance during his reign was the protracted but ruthlessly repressed Jewish revolt of 131 - 135 AD. It was provoked by his plan to build a new city with a temple dedicated to Jupiter on the site of Jerusalem. In Italy his buildings included the Pantheon and his mausoleum (now the Castel Sant' Angelo at Rome), and the magnificent villa at the popular resort of Tibur, filled with architectural reproductions of the wonders he had seen on his travels. Many other cities in the Empire benefited from Hadrian's passion for building or from generous government funding for their own projects. One of the emperors more unusual foundations was the city of Antinoopolis on the Nile. It commemorated the drowning in the river of his young favorite, Antinous, during an Imperial tour of Egypt. The grief stricken Emperor ordered that divine honors should be paid to Antinous. Gold statues of the young man, depicted as various gods, were raised all over the Empire.

After Hadrian's death the Senate was slow to deify him. Relations between the Emperor and the Senate had never been very cordial since early in his reign, when Hadrian was establishing his claim to the Imperial throne and four senators were executed in obscure circumstances. Hadrian's adopted son and chosen successor, Antoninus, threatened to refuse the throne unless the Senate promptly deified Hadrian – a stance that earned him the name Antoninus Pius. The fact that the Senate gave way illustrates the extent to which emperors now seemed indispensable, even in the eyes of the former masters of the Republic. The reign of Antoninus Pius from 138 to 161 AD was blissfully uneventful, and later generations looked back on it as a golden age. Any uprisings on the fringes of the Empire were for the moment easily contained. In Britain, the frontier was extended by the building of the Antonine Wall.

Antoninus' successor, Marcus Aurelius, was less fortunate: made for peace, he spent most of his reign with the armies in the East or in the Danube region. The empire itself experienced a number of calamities. Becoming Emperor within a few weeks of his 40th birthday, Marcus had been groomed for office by Hadrian, and during Antoninus' lifetime he had acquired a wealth of administrative experience. On his accession Marcus chose not to reign alone. He appointed a co-Emperor, Lucius Verus – the first indication that the burden of Empire might be becoming too heavy for a single man, except in very favorable circumstances. After Verus's death in 169 A.D. the experiment was suspended. In the campaigns of 162 - 165 AD, Verus repelled the Parthians and recaptured the province of Mesopotamia. Unfortunately his victorious army brought back home from the East a plague that swept through the Empire and inflicted serious damage on its population, economy and morale. The full extent of the damage may never be known, although some historians have speculated that Rome may never have completely recovered from it. Meanwhile multiple fierce German tribes poured across the Danube and even penetrated northern Italy and the Balkans. After more than a decade of hard campaigning, interrupted by a revolt in Syria and other worries, Marcus defeated the Germanic tribes so thoroughly that Rome seemed on the point of acquiring a large new German province when Marcus died.

Marcus's warlike career was not one that he would have chosen: paradoxically, he was the only Roman Emperor who was also a philosopher. He adhered to the Stoic school, which emphasized self-sufficient virtue, the endurance of necessary evils and the fulfillment of worldly duties – principles that doubtless strengthened his resolve to remain at his post. Marcus Aurelius's notebook, published as his Meditations, is a classic account of the mind striving to reconcile itself to the conditions of existence. But Marcus had a son; and his philosophy did not prevent him from violating the Antonine principle of selecting the best man for the job: instead, he chose as his successor his son Commodus, who was quite possibly the worst man.

Even less admirable than Nero, Commodus was obsessed with gladiatorial displays and himself fought regularly in the arena. His father Marcus Aurelius had dedicated the last years of his life to pacify the Rhine and Danube borders, but Commodus had little interest in wars. At the beginning of his reign, anxious to return to Rome, he made a hasty peace with the German tribes. It is reputed to that he was debauched, avaricious, and cruel. He was so convinced of his physical prowess that he believed that he was the reincarnation of Hercules – a number of statues show him masquerading as Hercules in a lion skin and carrying a club. Subsequently peace was maintained in the Empire, but life in Rome reverted to the familiar pattern of treason trials engendering conspiracies that engendered more treason trials – until Commodus was strangled by an athlete hired for the purpose by his own inner circle.

'If a man were called to fix the period in the history of the world, the condition of the human race was most happy and prosperous, he would, without hesitation, name that which elapsed from the death of Domitian to the accession of Commodus.' So wrote Edward Gibbon, author of the monumental, enduring Decline and Fall of the Roman Empire, published between 1776 and 1788. There is still something to be said in favor of his opinion, provided 'the human race' is assumed to consist of affluent citizens, excluding among others slaves and barbarians. Despite what was happening on the frontiers, most of the Empire was happy and prosperous. Towns flourished and civic amenities became ever more generous. An efficient system of roads brought the provinces together. Agriculture and industry prospered everywhere. Taxation was light. The number of citizens was greatly increased throughout the Empire, and the admission of provincials to the Senate made it far more representative than in the past; consequently many of the inhabitants of the Empire were beginning to think of it as a Commonwealth rather than an aggregation of Rome conquered territories. The civil service was staffed by the senatorial and equestrian classes, whose career opportunities reconciled them to the loss of their old political and judicial functions. And there was even a cultural revival – notably a silver age of literature, not quite comparable with the Augustine Golden age but still able to nurture such figures as the poets Juvenal and Martial, the romance writer Apuleius, the historians Tacitus and Suetonius, the elegant letter writer Pliny the Younger, and Greek authors like the biographer Plutarch and the satirist Lucian of Samosata.

Gibbon identified the flaw in the Antonine scheme of things: 'the instability of a happiness which depended on the character of a single man'. But there were others too, less obvious, which came to light as soon as the single man lost his power or his sanity. Despite state assistance, the Italian smallholders were being driven to the wall by the large slave operated estates. Compelling the Imperial government to make more and more decisions and develop an increasingly large, and potentially rigid and inefficient bureaucracy. The use of local troops to defend the frontiers risked the development of provincial loyalties and the possibility of secessions as soon as the grip of the central authority slackened; and the employment of barbarian auxiliaries settled within the frontier was potentially even more dangerous.

The potential weaknesses rapidly became actual with the madness and death of Commodus. The age of the Antonines ended, and the Roman empire plunged into a series of crises more serious than any it had known since the foundation of the principate.

Chapter 10: Rome in Crisis

Roman emperors generally tried to give their autocratic power some appearance of legitimacy. Augustus did it by respecting traditional forms and pretending to be no more than princeps – first man in the state; the less stable emperors among his successors spoiled the illusion by capricious acts of tyranny that finally destroyed the dynasty. The Antonines gave Imperial rule firm moral basis: the Emperor was best man as well as first, visibly working hard and co-opting his successor of proven ability. The system broke down when Marcus Aurelius co-opted his irresponsible son Commodus. After Commodus' assassination the Senate chose a man from their group named Pertinax as Emperor. He was less fortunate than Nerva had been in a similar position 100 years before. Pertinax's economic practices angered the Praetorians, who murdered him and blatantly put the Empire up for sale. The highest bidder was one Didius Julianus; but he had hardly taken the throne when the Legions in the provinces took up arms, and went to war against one another. In the ensuing civil wars Didius Julianus perished, Lyons was sacked, and the leader of the Legions in Pannonia - Septimus Severus - finally emerged as the master of Rome.

Severus was a tough military man, and ruled as such. He had little time for the Senate, which had backed one of his rivals, and he kept the favor of the Army by increasing its pay. He also recognized military marriages, which had not been allowed in the whole period of professional soldiering since Marius' time, although this had not prevented unofficial unions from flourishing. After campaigning over much of the Empire, Severus arrived in Britain, fought an indecisive war against the Caledonians in the north, strengthened Hadrian's Wall, and died at York in 211 AD.

Severus was succeeded by his son Caracalla, ensured his own supremacy by having his brother murdered, but in other respects followed his father's advice. The armies pay was substantially increased, and to help meet the cost Roman citizenship was extended to all free men and the Empire making them liable to pay an inheritance tax. This completed the slow evolution of the Empire into a single, effectively uniform society where a man status, rank and class mattered more than his geographical origin.

Despite some respectable military achievements Caracalla was killed by his officers – a feat that was to become increasingly common for Roman emperors. The prestige of the Antonines was such that even in these violent times emperors changed their names to join the earlier dynasty, and some sort of legality was observed; but this broke down in about 230 AD, when utter chaos reigned. Of the long, long list of emperors and pretenders over the next 50 years, Decius is remembered as the first Emperor to launch a general persecution of the Christians.

Claudius II and Aurelian distinguished themselves by driving back the barbarians who were menacing the Empire. Claudius was spared human ingratitude when he died of the plague, but Aurelian, hailed as restitutor orbis (restorer of the world) became yet another victim of discontented or ambitious officers.

During this period it must have seemed that the Empire was on the verge of disintegration. Economic decline, most marked in the West, accompanied civil wars and devastating bouts of plague. The Franks and Alemanni broke through the frontiers and ravaged Gaul and northern Italy; Gothic barbarians took to the sea and looted the Aegean; Persia again became a great power, inspired by a new dynasty, the Sassanids. The general insecurity of the Empire showed itself in a new development, the building of defensive walls by municipalities including the Aurelian Wall. Rome had never before felt the need to defend itself at this kind of a scale. At one of the low points in Roman history, in 260 AD, the Emperor Valerian was captured by the Persians. This would prove to be a shattering blow to Roman prestige. Meanwhile Gaul, Britain and Palmyra became virtually independent and usurpers sprang up everywhere. However, between 268 and 275 AD, Claudius II and Aurelian restored the military situation to order. In 284 AD when their fellow-Illyrian Diocletian was proclaimed as Emperor by the troops in the East, he set himself the task of reorganizing the Empire from top to bottom.

The Emperor Diocletian saved the state, but at a cost: he turned it into an Oriental despotism, served by a rigid bureaucracy, in a society increasingly organized on caste lines. For the most part these measures have been foreshadowed by existing tendencies in the Roman state. The Emperor for example was already an object of religious veneration, and no longer considered the first man, but instead the Lord. Diocletian took matters to their logical conclusion by separating himself from the populace, identifying himself with Jupiter, and emphasizing his semi-divine nature through elaborate ceremonial rituals. Similarly, the fiction that the Emperor needed Senatorial approval was finally abandoned and all civil service posts were thrown open to senators and equestrians alike, ending the remaining distinctions within the ruling class.

For administrative purposes the Empire was organized into a dozen dioceses run by vicars – terms that were to survive as ecclesiastical divisions within the later Christian church. Military and civil functions were separated to make defense more efficient and slow down any separatist tendencies in the provinces. Dukes and counts were created and charged with the responsibility of repelling barbarian attacks. The Army was localized now more than ever. Peasant militias and barbarian auxiliaries who had settled down within the frontiers bore the brunt of attacks from outside.

They were assisted by smaller units of mobile regulars. Heavy cavalry rapidly became more important than the once invincible legions, in which the infantry had been the supreme arm. The badly depreciated currency was reformed and proved to be even less successful when market prices were fixed by government decree. Bureaucracy and taxation bore heavily on the peoples of the Empire, making municipal responsibilities even less attractive. Division became harder as an increasing number of offices and crafts were declared hereditary, compelling many sons to follow the same occupations as their fathers. It all sounds worse, perhaps, than it really was. In an insecure world any order may be better than none, and caste societies, however unattractive, have often proved to be extremely durable. In any event, much of Diocletian's work was to outlive him and to last as long as Empire itself.

There can be no doubt that Diocletian system was the creation of realism rather than megalomania, for he showed a remarkable willingness to share power and eventually to renounce it. Previous emperors had co-opted colleagues, but Diocletian tried to institutionalize the practice and give it a geographical basis. He promoted an old comrade-in-arms, Maximian, to co-Emperor and gave him the Western Empire to rule. The west-east boundary ran from the Danube to the Adriatic. Diocletian's creation, the tetrarchy, was completed by appointing a Caesar, or Junior Emperor, as the assistant and heir of each Augustus. Significantly, Diocletian reserved for himself the East, where wealthy cities continued to flourish. He set up his court at Nicomedia, strategically placed on the Bosporus. With Italy in an economic decline, Rome had lost much of her old importance, and Maximian made his headquarters at Milan. This was closer to the frontier areas where trouble might arise. Some of these arrangements proved temporary, but the realities that prompted them did not. The strength of the Empire was becoming concentrated in the East. The West was declining, and only the prestige attached to the name of Rome disguised the fact.

While Diocletian ruled, the system worked. In 305 AD, after 21 years on the throne, he abdicated – a voluntary act, unique in Imperial Roman history. The last 11 years of his life were spent at his enormous palace in Dalmatia, later the nucleus of the town of Spalato, where he planted gardens and studied philosophy. He reappeared briefly in 308 AD to preside over an attempt to sort out the tangled affairs of the Empire. Maximian, the Caesars, and their relations were already battling furiously amongst themselves, but Diocletian's system was already beyond repair. The constant bickering and political intrigue went on long after Diocletian's death. It lasted until Constantine, the son of Maximian's first Caesar, emerged as sole victor.

In 306 AD, Constantius I Chlorus ruled in the western part of the Empire. He was formerly a Caesar and was now co-Emperor. He and his son Constantine crossed to Britain and drove back an invasion by the untamed tribes north of Hadrian's Wall. When Constantius died suddenly at York, Constantine was hailed as Emperor by his troops and became a Caesar, controlling Gaul and Britain, in a reconstituted tetrarchy. Six years of military and political intrigues followed, until in 312 AD Constantine was strong enough to invade Italy, defeat his rival Maxentius at the Milvian Bridge, and become Emperor of the West.

    Constantine favored Christianity from at least this time, by contrast with earlier emperors who had looked to the old Roman religion to restore the old Roman virtues. Diocletian, for example, had persecuted Christianity during his last years. By the edict of Milan in 1313 AD, Constantine and the Emperor in the East, Licinius, proclaimed general toleration of Christians. They also declared that confiscated Christian property should be returned. Later Licinius began to persecute Christians, perhaps because their religion had become politically identified with Constantine. War broke out, Licinius was defeated, and by 324 AD Constantine was master of a reunited Roman world.

Christians were far more numerous in the East, and Constantine could now safely lavish his patronage on the church. Having long made way against Imperial indifference or active hostility, Christianity flourished throughout Constantine's reign, no doubt gaining strength as doubters realized that it did not involve un-Roman weaknesses such as pacifism. By the end of Constantine's reign Christianity was effectively the state religion, although it was not as yet persecuting its rivals.

Constantine's greatest material legacy was a new capitol, begun in 326 and dedicated in 330 on the site of the old Greek city of Byzantium. New Rome, which was soon to become known as Constantinople, the city of Constantine, was planned as a Christian capitol; although pagan as well as Christian ceremonies were discreetly allowed at its foundation, no pagan temples were built within its walls. The site was superbly chosen – the end of a small peninsula on the European coast of the Bosporus where it joins the sea of Marmara. Surrounded on three sides by the sea, it became near impregnable when immensely strong walls were built across the peninsula. Indentations on the coastline provided good harbors, and a long inlet (the Golden Horn) was large enough to shelter a Navy. It was narrow enough for defenders to keep enemy ships out by stringing chains across the entrance. The city controlled the natural land route from Europe to Asia, as well as the sea route from the Mediterranean into the Black Sea. It served as a well-placed headquarters for an Empire that was most strongly menaced from across the Danube and the Tigris. Constantine's choice, not so very far from Nicomedia, confirmed Diocletian's wisdom in making the East the new heart of the Empire.

Constantinople would be a Christian Imperial city for the next 1,100 years.

In many other respects Constantine furthered Diocletian's work. The Imperial bureaucracy grew still larger and it was equipped with ever wider powers and duties; the separation between civil and military powers became complete; the admission of barbarians as Army recruits continued; taxation remained onerous, and measures were taken to prevent peasants from leaving the land and the wealthy were motivated toward municipal office. The attempt to create a rigid but stable society had some success; for although the value of the old silver denarius continued to depreciate there was at least a partial economic recovery, mainly thanks to the introduction of the new coin, the gold solidus. And by favoring the new Christian faith, Constantine promoted an ideology that was to prove effective in increasing social cohesion and would long outlive the Empire in the world of late antiquity.

Chapter 11: End of the Empire

After Constantine's death in 337, his sons and nephews allowed neither their blood ties nor the Christian faith to hinder them from murdering one another. Ironically, the last survivor of the family was Constantine's half nephew Julian, a passionate classicist who attempted during his brief reign to revive the worship of the old gods, maintaining a policy of toleration shifting state patronage and funding from churches to temples. In 363 Julian died while campaigning against a revived Persian Empire before his religious policy could have much of an effect; having been raised as a Christian and freely rejected the faith, Julian was long reviled as the apostate. With the extinction of Constantine's line the Army chose to support one of Julian's senior officers, Jovian, who made a hasty peace with Persia and restored Christianity as the religion of the Empire before dying in 364 AD.

The next Army-made Emperor, Valentinian, appointed his brother Valens co-Emperor and ruler of the East. From this time onwards West and East were effectively, though not officially, separate realms. Valentinian was an able general, and he was constantly on the move from the Danube to Britain. He was occupied with barely successful efforts to repel invaders and mend breaches in the frontier defenses. The first decisive break down occurred in the East, just three years after Valentinian's death, when a Germanic people, the Visigoths, crossed the Danube into the Empire. Ironically, they arrived not as invaders but as refugees from ferocious Central Asian nomads, the Huns, whose crushing victories and savage behavior set the entire barbarian world on the move. After initially friendly reception, the Visigoths were so carelessly handled by the Romans that they took to arms, ravaged the Balkans, and then, in 378 AD, defeated and killed the Emperor Valens at the battle of Adrianople. A new Eastern Emperor, Theodosius, failed to defeat the intruders but managed to pacify them and settle them in Thrace as military allies. The precarious situation of the Empire was now clear. Frightened and formidable barbarian tribes were fleeing the terrible Huns and approaching the frontier borders at a time when the Romans could no longer rely on their military superiority over them. Indeed, Roman armies were increasingly manned by other imported barbarians, creating a situation in which the distinction between defenders and invaders became easily obscured.

Theodosius restored order in the East and intervened in the West to place the youthful Valentinian II back on his throne. Underneath the fervently devout and Orthodox Theodosius, the future of Christianity as an exclusive state religion began to take shape: Arians along with other heretics had been persecuted and the pagan temples were closed or taken over. Within the final months of his life, having invaded Italy and overthrowing the usurping warlord,

Arbogast, Theodosius became the only ruler of the Empire. He was the last: and in 395 AD his dominions had been divided between his sons Arcadius and Honorius, and although the division had no unique importance at the time, it turned out to be permanent.

In the West, things soon began to fall apart. The Visigoths became restless again, while Vandals, Alans, and other people poured into Gaul. Only the ability of a barbarian general in Roman pay, the Vandal Stilicho, had given much hope that Rome could hold on; but Stilicho's behavior was ambiguous and in 408 AD his son-in-law, the Emperor Honorius, became fearful of his general's intentions and had him murdered. Britain was effectively abandoned at this time; it was the second fully Romanized province to be lost. Then, in 410 AD, the Visigoths under Alaric sacked Rome itself. The city had been replaced as the Imperial capitol in the late third century, and had been eclipsed by Constantinople; but the name of Rome is still redolent of past glories, and for Roman citizens everywhere its sack was a symbol and a psychological catastrophe of the first order. The Visigoths moved through France into Spain, driving the Vandals in front of them: the Vandals crossed into North Africa, from where they were later to sack Rome with a gleeful thoroughness that has made their name a byword for mindless destruction.

Imperial recognition of the barbarian Spanish and African kingdoms amounted to an admission that they were no longer part of the Empire. But there were still times at which it seemed that something might be salvaged. The Huns plundered the Western Empire but were driven out of Gaul, bought off or bluffed out Italy, and then, after the death of Attila, broke up – to the relief of the Romans and other barbarian peoples alike. But the Vandal sack of Rome followed three years later in 455 AD. The history of the West became a shambles in which the emperors were often no more than the puppets of Roman barbarian generals. The last Western

Emperor, Romulus Augustus, was the most grandiosely named; in spite of which he was deposed on the 4th of September 476 AD after reigning for only a year, and the Roman Empire in the West came to an end. For a time Romulus Augustus's barbarian successors kept up the fiction that they were representatives of the Eastern Empire, but by 490 AD Italy had become ruled by another group of Germanic people, the Ostrogoths, who then set up their own entirely independent kingdom.

The great folk wanderings were far from over, but the likely outcome was already apparent: the Empire was dead, but the barbarians would eagerly accept the religion of Rome and as much as they could assimilate of its culture, which they admired even as their activities helped it to crumble all around them.

The East was terribly battered by the events of the fifth century, but it managed to survive thanks to its greater resources, the strong laws of Constantinople, and especially the subtlety displayed by its emperors in playing off barbarian armies against one another. The reign of Justinian from 527 to 565 AD witnessed a recovery so brilliant that for a few years it even seemed that the Mediterranean might again become a Roman Lake: North Africa and, much more arduously, Italy were recovered by Justinian's generals Belisarius and Narses, and the southeast of Spain was conquered from the Visigoths. Justinian had a genius for being well served – and even well partnered, for his wife Theodora, a former actress whose past may have been more than a little shady, proved to be a strong-willed and politically capable Empress; it was her firm stand that dissuaded Justinian from fleeing when the Nika riots of 532 AD threatened to turn into a revolution. Justinian himself was an able administrator who reformed and purged the civil service, though his ambitious policies still put a great strain on the Empire's resources. Like Constantine he had a powerful voice in the affairs of the church, although he too failed to reconcile the hostile factions, while quarreling over whether Jesus had a single or dual nature.

One of Justinian's greatest achievements was to preside over a codification of the law that ultimately influenced Western Europe even more than the East. Above all he initiated a great building program throughout the empire; at Constantinople it was crowned by the completion of the church of St. Sophia, whose domed splendor cause Justinian to cry out "Solomon, I have surpassed thee!" There was even a literary revival, although not all its manifestations can have pleased the Emperor: Procopius, the court historian, took his revenge within the constraints of official record making by compiling a Secret History, which he filled with very rude stories about the Imperial family.

Justinian's reconquest of Italy was completed in 554 AD; but only 14 years later a new people, the Lombards, overran much of the Peninsula. Rome remained technically under Imperial control, but the city's new rulers were its bishops, then called popes. With new doctrines and structures developing in the old Imperial capitol, and the Eastern Empire becoming increasingly Greek in character, during the sixth century the history of ancient Rome can reasonably be said to have come to an end.

Conclusion

In the centuries following Justinian's death in 565 AD, the Byzantine Empire ebbed and flowed, intermittently gaining control of territory in Italy. For the most part, the Empire was restricted to the Balkans in modern Turkey. Rome had become something of a backwater, as its population plummeted to just tens of thousands, a far cry from the height of the Empire when more than 1 million people crammed into the city.

  Justinian's war against the Ostrogoths had ravaged the Italian peninsula. After the Byzantines in the Ostrogoths were pushed out, the Lombards, a Germanic people from northern Europe, moved in. The Lombards did little to regenerate Italy, and were eventually ousted by the Franks, another Germanic tribe, at the end of the eighth century. The Frankish King, Charlemagne, was rewarded with the title

Emperor of the Romans by the Pope, and became the first of the holy Roman emperors.

After Charlemagne's death, his territories were split in half, with the Franks continuing to control the area of Roman Gaul, and the Holy Roman Empire being carved out of northern Italy and Germany.

The creation of a Holy Roman Empire was partly an attempt to rekindle the Western Roman Empire. The emperors were appointed by the Pope, and they ruled over vast swathes of central Europe for almost a millennium, until Napoleon reorganized the region in 1806. However, the Holy Roman Empire was really quite different to the Roman Empire; it was a confederation of small states and principalities, and it was centered on Germany, neither of which had been true of ancient Rome.

The Byzantine Empire continued on in the Roman Empire in the East for many centuries. Over time it grew gradually weaker as new, powerful tribes moved into the region under the banner of Islam. At times only Constantinople's near impenetrable walls kept the city safe from seemingly imminent destruction. The city was sacked in 1204 AD during the fourth Crusade, which set in motion a steady decline as the population plummeted. Two and a half centuries later, in 1453 AD, Constantinople finally fell to the Ottomans and the Byzantine Empire passed into history.

In the West, Italy remained divided for centuries, ownership of the land being carved up between foreign invaders, wealthy families, and the Catholic Church. After a series of wars in a conscious nationalist effort, Italy was reunified during the 19th century. Much of the reunification task was completed by 1861, but Rome still remained elusive because it was under papal control, backed by French support. Paris finally removed its backing in 1870 and Italian troops took the city. Italy was finally unified as a nation; Rome was established as the capitol, and it was once again placed at the heart of the short-lived empire, ruling over parts of Africa, the Balkans, and Greece.

The array of fascinating Roman relics that litter Europe, North Africa and the Middle East strike off into the millions that visit in each year. But the Romans have bequeathed so much more to us than just ruined buildings; we continue to be influenced by Roman politics, law, time, literature, town planning, sanitation and road building. Even Roman education and medicine, which are now largely discredited, were upheld until very recently. The political systems of the Roman Republic have influenced the American and French systems among many others, and the word Caesar was still evident in the German Kaiser and Russia Czar until these positions were abolished during the first world war. The Romans were also largely responsible for the removal of the Jews from Judea, an act that was to have fateful consequences in the 20th century, in which still impacts international relations to this day.

One of Rome's greatest legacies is its language; Latin forms the root of a number of European languages, including Italian, French, Portuguese, Spanish, and Romanian. Even the Germanic English language, that has replaced Latin as the language of trade of our time, owes much of its vocabulary to Latin words. Rome's other greatest legacy is religion; since Jesus's disciple, St. Peter, was crucified in the city, Rome became an important religious center of the Christian church. The Bishop of Rome, later called the Pope, could claim to be the successor of St. Peter, which meant that through the centuries he retained an important role, despite the relegation of Rome to the sidelines.

Over time, theological and political differences led to a split between the Christian churches of the East and West and the Pope became the highest authority of the Western, Catholic Church. Today the Catholic Church has the most followers of all the world's religions; one in every six people is a member of the

Catholic Church. At the heart of such a massive religion, the city of Rome has been able to retain its position at the center of the world, long after the Roman empire disappeared.

By the end of the fifth century A.D. the Roman Empire in the west lay in ruin. Many new peoples and Kingdoms had risen up and were busy occupying its former territories. The Roman civilization managed to live on, both materially and spiritually. In the East, Emperors still continued to hold court in Constantinople; the Byzantine Roman Empire increasingly became seen as a medieval land that was very different from ancient Rome – a factor historians have since acknowledged by renaming it the Byzantine Empire. In this form it deeply influenced the neighboring Slav peoples. It evolved into the Christian identity that eventually separated its church from the Roman Catholic church in the West. Meanwhile vigorous societies arose in Western Europe. They possessed values, customs and arts of their own, but they remained over-awed by the achievements of the Romans, repeatedly looked back inside to learn from them, and viewed many of their own great movements as partly involving a return to classical values. Even the modern mind, however culturally independent, is saturated by words, thoughts and images that originated with the extraordinary civilization of ancient Rome.

Catastrophes aside, there are few clean-cut endings in history. The last Emperor in the West was forcibly retired, but in the East the Roman Empire went on without Rome. However the East Romans who spoke Greek are not the people we normally mean when we talk of the ancient Greeks and Romans; and historians have generally agreed to distinguish between the East Roman Empire of late antiquity and what is now known as the Byzantine Empire, which belongs to the history of the Middle Ages. The reign of Justinian makes a convenient watershed, although some historians defer the transition from Roman to Byzantine until the disastrous seventh century. This is when the Arabs who were inspired by the doctrines of Islam swept out of the Arabian Peninsula and conquered the Eastern and North African provinces, which became part of a huge new Muslim Empire that stretched from Spain to India.

From this time onwards the heartland of the Byzantine Empire was Anatolia, with more or less precarious extensions in the Balkans in Italy. The Empire was beset from West and East by Slavic and Islamic enemies, and much of its subsequent history represents a struggle for survival. Even so, Byzantine wealth, luxury and culture were the astonishment of barbarians, both West European and sloth: the wonders of Constantinople, the size and splendor of its palaces and churches, and its mechanical and military marvels including the famous Greek fire, a sort of Molotov cocktail had a great deal to do with the conversion of slots to Christianity. Unwilling to defer to a barbarian Rome,

Byzantine Christianity asserted its independence, ultimately emerging as the Eastern Orthodox Church, which still commands the allegiance of most Slav and Greek Christians. Byzantium produced a flourishing Greek literature, a Greek version of Roman legal codes, and a splendid and opulent art which found expression in illuminated manuscripts, wall painting, mosaics, ivories, metalwork and enameling.

From the ninth to the 11th century the Empire was at its height; but then disaster struck. The Normans expelled Byzantines from southern Italy; and in 1071 the Byzantine Army – prudently nurtured and conserved for centuries by a limited risk strategy – was shattered at the battle of Manzikert by a new people, the Seljuk Turks. Manzikert, and the loss of Anatolia, where blows from which the Byzantines never properly recovered. Help arrived from Western Europe in the form of Crusaders, but Latins and Greeks did not get along, and during the fourth Crusade it was the Crusader Latins, not the Turks, who stormed and took Constantinople for the first time in its history. Within half a century most of the Latins had been driven out, and the Empire was noticeably in decline. A new Turkish people, the Ottomans, surged into Asia minor and on to the Balkans, bypassing a beleaguered Constantinople, and during its last years Byzantium was little more than an Ottoman vassal state. The storming of Constantinople in 1453 – nominally the end of one of the great epochs of world history – was almost an anti-climax. However, the heritage of ancient Greece and Rome lived on.

The posthumous influence of ancient Rome has no parallel in history. The barbarians who had almost unintentionally brought down the Empire marveled at what was left behind and imitated it as well as they could. For centuries any advance in Western civilization was equated with the restoration of Roman institutions, styles and values. In 800 AD, the Frankish king

Charlemagne was finally crowned Emperor by the Pope; in effect Charlemagne was perceived as a new Roman Emperor, and essentially the European Holy Roman Empire remained on the map for the next thousand years. The uneasy relationship between Holy Roman Emperors and popes was a central issue in medieval politics. As the Bishop of Rome, the pope was also a successor to the Roman Emperors, deriving part of his authority from his position in the old world capitol. Struggling to re-create civilization, men like Charlemagne could think of nothing better than to imitate antiquity – sometimes in literal reproduction like Aachen Cathedral, which is San Vitale, Ravenna, with some refinements absent. Rulers in the Dark Ages continue to use the main Roman unit of currency, the solidus, and copied it when they became confident enough to mint their own coins. The literature and learning of the ancient world is largely preserved through the efforts of monks, who wish to preserve the heritage of civilization despite their suspicion of pagan author's morals and messages; and the earliest attempts to create a Christian Drama was undertaken by a Saxon nun who produced sanitized versions of Terence's comedies for convent use.

The first great European style of architecture betrays its affinities in its name: Romanesque. In its 12th century successor, Gothic, Europeans last produced a great style the old little to the classic past; but intellectually they were still dependent on Roman and Greek authorities. Everywhere in the medieval East, Latin was the language of learning, law, theology, diplomacy in debate, although long since dead as the vernacular of the people. Remarkably, when new intellectual and artistic preoccupations appeared with the Renaissance, they were mainly expressed in terms of a renewed cult of antiquity. Petrarch, like the Roman poets, was laurel crowned on the capitol. The Dutch satirist Erasmus polished his Latin style through the study of Cicero. Architects studied the Roman author Vitruvius and built domed churches and country villas. Artists like Michelangelo were inspired by Roman copies of Greek masterpieces. Beginning in Italy, the Renaissance spread out over Europe, taking various forms; its promotion of Latin literature influenced everything from poetic metre to the four act play, and made Virgil and Ovid major influences on European writers from Dante to Shakespeare and beyond.

In the 16th and 17th centuries the vocabulary of art remain classical, although the Mannerist and Baroque movements put it to uses that would have outraged the Greeks and Romans. The 18th century however brought the first extensive discoveries at Pompeii and Herculaneum, inspiring a new version of the antique, neo-classicism, which transformed interior decoration and placed a little temple in the grounds of every country house or Roman style villa.

At the end of the 18th century the hold of antiquity seemed as strong as ever. Rousseau's

Du Contrat Social, often regarded as the textbook of the French Revolutionaries, discussed political problems almost entire in terms of Greek and Roman history. The revolutionaries themselves, people inspired by neo-classical painting, aped Brutus and Cato. Napoleon, First Consul and Emperor of France, borrowed elements as well. With his "Legion de Honour", Arc de Triomphe, and Eagles, he was even more conscious of playing a heroic-antique role.

Even the replacement of Latin by vernacular languages, the rise of science and the advent of the Industrial Revolution failed to shake the hold of classical antiquity on the western mind. For better or worse, in the 19th century Greek and Latin remained central to upper class education, and classicism in art and architecture came to represent a rejection of the new. Consequently the reaction against Victorianism also affected attitudes towards the classical past; some people still think of it as dull, although blockbuster films have done a great deal to cure that. Now, technology and post-modernism may – arguably – have made the Roman heritage irrelevant; but it remains obstinately embedded in contemporary language and ideas. Rome is featured in films such as Gladiator, Spartacus, Cleopatra, Ben-Hur, and more. Elements of Roman history have been adapted for television programs, like HBO's hit series Rome. The ghost of ancient Rome lives on even through the Las Vegas Casino, Caesar's Palace. Senates, capitols and dictators are still with us, and in our time Apollo has landed on the Moon and Mars beckons.

Great advances have been made in recent years in learning more about Roman life. While tragedies in themselves, the ruins of cities like Pompeii and Herculaneum have given modern researchers an inside look at the diets, habits, and daily life of Roman citizens. The site of Pompeii consists of 160 acres, of which nearly two thirds remains yet to be excavated. Part of this is done because of funding, but primarily as an attempt to preserve the city from further deterioration. The volcanic material that covered the city of Pompeii helped the city remain intact until present day. The belongings of the people were largely preserved, still in their homes and shops for archaeologists to discover. This has allowed modern researchers to study architecture, art, as well as ancient city design. Surprisingly, significant amounts of paintings, including wall frescoes, were preserved. Magnificent mosaic floors remained, which in nearly any other city would have been destroyed by invaders or the passage of time. The amphitheater, multiple temples, entire districts of homes, and even a gladiator school remain for modern researchers to study. Interest in ancient peoples has resurfaced, and through studying what was left behind, we discover that they aren't so different from us after all.

Other books available by author on Kindle, paperback and audio

Hannibal Barca, The Greatest General: The Meteoric Rise, Defeat, and Destruction of Rome's Fiercest Rival

History's Greatest Military Commanders: The Brilliant Military Strategies of Hannibal, Alexander The Great, Sun Tzu, Julius Caesar, Napoleon Bonaparte, And 30 Other Historical Commanders

Made in the USA
Coppell, TX
09 March 2021